BACKYARD
ADVENTURE

BACK YARD ADVENTURE

51 FREE-PLAY ACTIVITIES

Get **MESSY**, Get **WET**, Build **COOL THINGS**, and Have **TONS OF WILD FUN!**

Amanda Thomsen

Storey Publishing

The mission of Storey Publishing is to serve our customers by publishing practical information that encourages personal independence in harmony with the environment.

Edited by Carleen Madigan
Art direction and book design by
    Jessica Armstrong
Text production by Jennifer Jepson Smith

Cover and interior photography © Kourtney
    Sellers
Additional interior photography by Courtesy
    of Amanda Thomsen, 9, 12, 16, 17, 61 top
    left, 68 top left, 114 left, 149, 154 bottom;
    © DERO2084/iStock.com, 89 giant hogweed;
    © Digital Paradise/Shutterstock.com, 89
    maple leaves; © Dow the garden path/Alamy
    Stock Photo, 23 bottom left; © Elizabeth
    Winterbourne/Shutterstock.com, 89 grasses;
    © Elena Srubina/Shutterstock.com, 89 ferns;
    © FamVeld/iStock.com, 26; © Gelpi/Shutter-
    stock.com, 88; © James Stockwin/Alamy
    Stock Photo, 23 top left; © jikgoe/iStock.com,
    89 lamb's ears; © John_Wijsman/iStock.com,
    89 poison ivy; © KatieDobies/iStock.com, 89
    mullein; © keith morris/Alamy Stock Photo, 23
    middle right; © Kylbabka/Shutterstock
    .com, 89 glossy leaves; © Linda Kennedy/
    Alamy Stock Photo, 23 bottom right; Mars
    Vilaubi, 62, © mirina/iStock.com, 68 top right;
    © Orchidpoet/iStock.com, 68 bottom left;
    © Radist/iStock.com, 27, © resulmuslu/iStock
    .com, 89 stinging nettle; © Tim ST Jones/
    Alamy Stock Photo, 23 top right; © Whiteway/
    iStock.com, 89 burdock
Illustrations by Ilona Sherratt

Text © 2019 by Amanda Thomsen

Storey books are available for special pre-mium and promotional uses and for customized editions. For further information, please call 800-793-9396.

Storey Publishing
210 MASS MoCA Way
North Adams, MA 01247
storey.com

Printed in China by R.R. Donnelley
10 9 8 7 6 5 4 3 2 1

Library of Congress Cataloging-in-Publication Data on file

CONTENTS

CHAPTER ONE

FORTS AND OTHER HIDEAWAYS

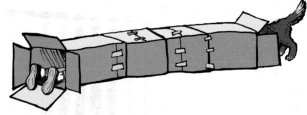

CHAPTER TWO

PLACES FOR TINKERING

CHAPTER THREE

NATURALLY WILD

Grow, Eat, Launch, Explore, Create

CHAPTER FOUR

SETTING UP CAMP

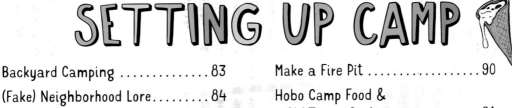

CHAPTER FIVE

SIDEWALKS, FENCES, AND DRIVEWAYS

A.K.A. Places to Draw

CHAPTER SIX
ADVENTURE COURSE

CHAPTER SEVEN
WATER, BUBBLES, AND GOO

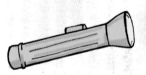

CHAPTER EIGHT
IT AIN'T OVER YET

SUPER SECRET SECTION
★ FOR PARENTS ONLY! ★ 149

THE ROOTS OF A WILD CHILD

My strongest childhood memories from growing up in the suburbs of Chicago are of the relentless, everyday boredom that reliably gave way to unbelievably creative, noisy, messy, and usually outdoor play.

I remember eating breakfast and then breaking out the back door like a racehorse and not coming in unless it was absolutely necessary. My parents would set peanut butter and jelly sandwiches out on the back stoop for me like I was some kind of feral grade-schooler.

One day when I ran out of ideas for what to do, this magical set of books appeared — *Making Things: The Handbook of Creative Discovery* by Ann Wiseman. I don't know where they came from or who the intended audience for these books was. (The set didn't seem like it was for kids and it was too simple for adults.) But for me, reading them was an almost religious experience. They were quirkily hand drawn, with super hippie block print spelling out ideas for weird crafts. From simple projects like weed weaving (reimagined and included in this book on page 30) and making things from old tin cans (which, I now realize, would surely create a bloodbath if carried out by little kids) to baking incredibly elaborate breads that looked like animals (and would never, ever fit in a normal oven), Wiseman's ideas just set my tiny brain ablaze. I can't even say that I actu-

My daughter, Hazel (pictured above in 2015), has as much fun playing in the yard as I did when I was her age. That's me, in the lower photo, circa 1979.

ally completed a single project from the books, but they were the fuel for years of play afterward. These books gave me inspiration, goals, and constant, everlasting weird dreams about bread animals.

I can only hope that kids and parents pick up this book and feel half of what I felt about the Ann Wiseman volumes. I hope it inspires children of all ages to unplug, put on some play clothes, get dirty, and explore. I'd love to hear about your messy outdoor adventures, too. You can call me up on a phone made out of an old tin can and tell me all about them, toll free!

CHAPTER ONE

FORTS
and OTHER HiDeaways

WE ALL WANT A PLACE OF OUR OWN — A PLACE WHERE WE CAN BE IN CHARGE. In your own little lair or tiny animal den, you get to be the rule maker and the decider. You can make a little hiding place that's all yours, one that you build and decorate however you like. How you build it depends on what kind of material you have lying around, but here are some tips to get started and a few ideas to build on.

Unplug, get outside, and make discoveries!

Scrounging for Unexpected
BUILDING MATERIALS

Before you can build, you need construction materials.

"Loose parts" are those magical items that you can play with and turn into whatever you want them to be. An old tire could become a spaceship. A box could be a time machine! A long length of PVC pipe could be a flagpole, part of a tent, a measuring device, a megaphone, a pea shooter, a tunnel, or a hose. I could go on and on, but I'm sure you'll have your own great ideas.

Visiting junkyards, reuse centers, and thrift stores for bits and pieces can spur new ideas for materials, but it is important to adhere to a budget even if the original plans go out the window. Junior junkers should also consider transportation of found items. Important questions include, "How will I get this home?" "Will it fit in the car?" "Will it mess up the car?"

Hazel has her own budget to buy loose parts today.

Will she choose dainty, breakable housewares?

Will she choose bigger, rustier stuff?

LOOSE PARTS AND UNEXPECTED PLAYTHINGS

* **SHEETS OF FOAM INSULATION.**
These can be carved into anything, including bricks, walls, tombstones, counters, doors, and roofs.

* **CHUNKS OF LEFTOVER LUMBER.**
These can become building blocks, like an oversize version of Lincoln Logs or TinkerToys.

* **PALLETS.** These make great fort walls, roofs, and drawbridges. They can be used as a stage, an organizer for all the other loose parts, or as an imaginary jet. Work gloves are helpful if you're worried about splinters.

* **OLD TOOLS.** Having your own tools will help you avoid the hassle of having to raid a parent's tool box.

* **CANNING JARS.** These can be used to hold potions, insects, or bouquets; to drink from; and to make terrariums.

* **WIRES.** Old wires can be used to build time machines, robots, nests, radios, and other interstellar connections.

* **BUCKETS.** They can be sandcastle forms or step stools. You can fill them with water and set them outside in winter for icy building blocks.

* **CRATES.** Use these as giant bricks, or add a rope to turn one into a trailer for hauling.

* **PIPES AND FITTINGS.** These can be used to build a framework for any kind of hideout, especially tepees and tents.

* **BUILDING MATERIALS.** You can make structures out of old chimney pipes, shoe molding, bolts, wheels, bricks, and stones.

* **CASTERS.** These are great for making your own carts and wheelbarrows.

* **BIKE WHEELS.** Use wheels as gears or cogs. Turn a wheel to make something happen.

* **TIRES.** These can become building blocks or tunnel supports.

* **FABRIC.** A large piece of fabric can be used to cover hideouts, snuggle up, or lie down on. You can also pile stuff on it and drag it around.

* **CHICKEN WIRE.** This makes a good framework for all kinds of hideaways and a great base for weaving with pretty much anything. Use gloves to protect your hands from pokey ends.

FORTS & PLAYHOUSES

Parents: Keep Out!

You can make any old tool shed into your own private hideout! Fly your flag, hang some curtains, or set booby traps to keep intruders out. The two brothers below decked out their old play structure and turned it into a fort. Fun!

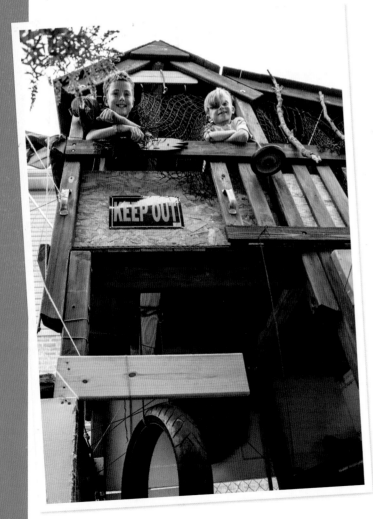

Play house or play fort —
take your pick!

NATURAL BURROWS

Let your yard go wild!

Choose an area (or the whole yard) and see what happens when it's left to grow as long as possible. Try burrowing through the grass and making a nest or a series of tunnels, as if you were a tiny mouse or a baby rabbit. Discover what happens when Mother Nature takes over as the designer.

Make a magical bouquet from wildflowers.

Is that Elsie or a wild tiger?

When I was little, my favorite place to play was an open space in the middle of three spruce trees that had been planted a little too close together, where the trees shed their needles (probably from lack of light). In this little hideaway, I had a wall-to-wall carpet of spruce needles, a drop in temperature because of the deep shade, cathedral ceilings, and all the coat racks a kid could want. And it was ready for play, 24/7/365.

Packing-Material TEPEE

One kind of play space you can make is a tepee.

We made one out of whatever we had lying around the house: Three 8-foot-long copper pipes, one 4-foot roll of chicken wire (it's sharp, so make sure you're wearing protective clothing and thick gloves when handling it!), parachute cord, zip ties, old bubble wrap, and clear packing tape. You can even build in stages and add bubble wrap as it arrives at your house in packages. No need to hurry!

There are lots of other options for building materials, too. You could build the tepee frame with PVC pipes, sticks, old lumber, or broomsticks. And you could cover it with: scraps of fabric tied to the chicken wire frame, a tarp, canvas, stuffed animals zip-tied to the chicken wire, old flip-flops, old homework, papier-mâché, or leaves and branches.

The tepee is quite a bit warmer inside, which makes building one a great late-autumn activity.

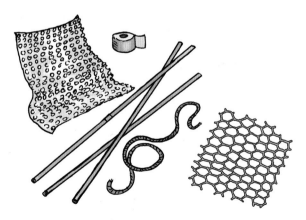

Is it a good size to play in?
I think so!

MAKE IT!

1 Lay the pipes down next to each other, weave rope between all three pieces at the top, and tie a knot. Do this at least twice, then pop up the structure.

2 Wrap one end of the chicken wire around one of the copper pipes and zip-tie it in place. Pull the chicken wire around your tepee form and zip-tie it to each pole, overlapping the chicken wire, if necessary. (Fold any extra chicken wire to make it lay flat, or snip off irregular pieces.)

3 Cut the chicken wire with wire cutters. Wearing gloves, bend the pointy ends in so you don't get snagged by them (ouch!). Cut a door opening into the chicken wire wherever you like. Bend all the jagged pieces of chicken wire back flat.

4 Cover the chicken wire with bubble wrap and clear tape. Make sure the bubble wrap covers the inside and outside edges of the doorway.

Plants That Make
GREAT PLACES TO HIDE

You can use nature to create a secret spot where you can hide, nap, or spy on your siblings.

Plants make great hiding spots. But some plants are sensitive and will get hurt if you play in them. Other plants aren't great for play because they have thorns or stickers, or can burn if someone brushes against them. Stinging nettles are an example of this.

Listed below are some fun plants for playing in that can take a beating (within reason!) and won't hurt anyone. They can be used solely for play or they can be used to create private nooks, as well as borders, fence-hiders, and even sound barriers. (Plants absorb sound, so the more plants, the less your neighbors can hear you. And the less you can hear your neighbors!)

* **SUNFLOWERS.** Plant them in a straight line to create a wall up to 12 feet tall.

* **TALL PERENNIAL GRASSES.** Try planting them in a large circle, or any other fun shape. You could even plant grasses so they spell out words! Sometimes you might get a little itchy when brushing by these grasses, but the itch doesn't last long.

* **EVERGREENS.** These create a play place for use all year long.

* **YARD-LONG BEANS.** This fast-growing vine will cover any kind of structure. The beans make great play weapons (and they taste good).

* **WEEPING WILLOWS.** These are the best outdoor toys I know of! You can swing on the branches or harvest them and use them to build other things (see page 22). Or you can create a large outdoor home within the weeping branches.

* **CORN.** It's fun to play in a farmer's cornfield, but once the corn is taller than the shortest kid playing, it can be very easy to get lost in it. Why not plant corn in your yard just for playing in? You'll have fun, and you'll still be able to find your little brother at the end of the day.

* **CATTAILS.** Usually these grow in shallow water, so make sure you wear rain boots if you find a patch of cattails to play in.

* **BAMBOO.** If you spot a grove of bamboo, it can be a bustling downtown that's filled with skyscrapers.

Build a
STRAW BALE FORT

Why not use straw bales as giant building blocks for a fort?

Will it have windows? A proper door, or just a hole to crawl through? Will you lay the bales flat or stack them on their ends? How many do you think you can stack? Will you draw a plan, like a blueprint, before you start building? Think about different roof types. You can use a tarp, a blanket, clear plastic sheeting, branches, cardboard, or an old window as a roof. Maybe you'll want no roof at all.

Hey, neighbor!

Engineering Tips

* Practice how you'll build your straw bale fort with blocks (or even shoe boxes) before you start working on the real thing. Make sure you leave space for a door.

* Don't stack them higher than you can reach. Straw bales are very heavy once they get wet, so moving them can be difficult.

Straw bales are so much heavier than you'd think!

Plant a
LIVING WILLOW HIDEAWAY

Growing your own living willow hideaway looks like it would be hard, but it really isn't.

For this project, you'll need about 20 straight willow branches, called "whips." If you don't have a willow in your yard you can forage branches from trees growing in roadside ditches (make sure you get permission first, though), or you can even purchase a package of whips. You should harvest whips and build your hideaway in the spring, before the trees begin to bud and leaf out. And you'll want to choose a sunny, moist spot to plant them.

MAKE IT!

1 Trace out a circle or just freestyle it!

Leave a space for the door.

2 Use a trowel to dig a hole in the ground for each whip. The holes should be about 8 inches deep, about 8 to 10 inches apart.

3 Place a whip in each hole and pack soil around them. Give them a bit of water.

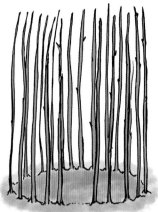

4 Weave the shoots together as the whips grow, or just bind them together at the top.

5 Trim off any overgrown shoots, and use the trimmings to start more living hideaways, or to replace any whips that didn't grow.

CARDBOARD CASTLES

A great activity the day before recycling pickup (or really anytime)!

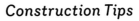

We like to order stuff online, so cardboard boxes pile up around here, waiting for recycling day. But if we get bored on a sunny Saturday afternoon, we tape them together to make a castle, a lair, or a hamster run of epic proportions. We leave our creations outside until they break down, and then use the cardboard remains to smother weeds in the garden. Worn-out cardboard castles can also be recycled or even composted. (Remove all plastic and tear the cardboard into smaller bits before throwing in the compost pile.)

Construction Tips

* Start with bigger boxes on the bottom and tape smaller boxes to the top.

* Open both ends of the box for extra height, then tape all around.

* Use flattened boxes as roofs.

* Duct tape is best for building, but clear packing tape works great, too.

* Serrated steak knives work well for cutting and are safer than box cutters (so slicey)! Ask an adult for permission.

ADD TO THE FUN: finger paints, crayons, markers, fun duct tape, papier-mâché paste, autumn leaves, blankets for relaxing, and a cooler full of healthy snacks

Painting the town red (and blue)!

A FORT IN WINTER

Winter definitely doesn't mean staying inside! Cross your fingers for snow and freezing temperatures so you can build your own winter playground.

ICE PALACE

Make an ice palace of your own design. Start by collecting all the cardboard milk and juice cartons you can find. In the fall, put the cartons outside in a hidden area, let nature fill them with water (and muck!), and when they are all frozen in the depths of winter, slide the ice blocks out of the cartons and use them as building blocks. Or you can fill the cartons with water indoors and set them outside to freeze. Depending on how cold the weather is, you'll have blocks in a few hours, but leaving them out overnight is best.

Experiment with different ways to hold a wall together. What's all around you that might be used as glue? (Hint: it's snow.) Which brick formations create the strongest walls?

OUTSIDE THE SNOW BANK IS SAFER

It might seem like the simplest way to make a snow structure is to tunnel into a pile of snow left behind by the snowplow. However, these can actually be dangerous places to burrow; a plow or other vehicle could easily hit the snowbank where you're playing, not knowing you're in there. It's safer to play outside of the snow bank rather than inside it.

Stack some chunks!

SNOWBALL IGLOO

Why not make an igloo with one million small snowballs (give or take a few)? Place the snowballs in a circle and continue to layer them up, working through your one million snowballs. Make sure to leave a door! As you layer up, you'll need to taper the circles, slightly, to create a domed roof.

If your snow is dry and breaks into pieces easily, you don't have to work as hard at making your building materials. Pull off chunks of snow, then stack them up, using handfuls of sloppier snow in between your "bricks" as cement. Remember: big chunks of snow are great for building, not for throwing at other kids!

SLEDDING WITHOUT A SLED

You don't have to have a store-bought sled to enjoy the snowfall. Here are some other items that make excellent sleds:

→ Cookie trays

→ Hubcaps

→ Tarps

→ Baby pools

→ Pieces of cardboard

→ Dry-cleaner bags

→ Plastic shower curtains

→ Clean oil drip pans

→ Old sturdy drawers

→ Outdoor seat cushions

→ Garbage can lids

→ Laundry baskets

→ Inflatable inner tubes

→ Plastic storage boxes (bonus: you can use the top or the bottom)

→ Old doors

TUNNELS

There's no telling what could be waiting at the other end once you crawl through! Is it a portal to another world? Is a fierce creature waiting on the other side?

Building a tunnel can be as simple as creating a low path through long tall grass. If the grass makes you too itchy, though, you can start with a premade play tunnel, like the ones sold by IKEA. Let the grass grow right over it all season, then cover it with leaves in autumn. Wrap or weave it with solar- or battery-powered string lights and it becomes an evening hangout.

Ideas for Tunnel Fun

* Cut the bottom out of a plastic garbage can to make a short tunnel.

* Bury the bottom quarter of a Hula-Hoop, then bury another one a few feet apart, and so on, until you have made a row. You can decide the direction you want it to go. Cover the hoops it however you like, with bubble wrap, old sheets, or tarps, and you'll have a tunnel.

* Use the same technique but with old tires. Bury them partially in the ground, then cover.

* Tape large broken down cardboard boxes end to end to make a tube.

How many different ways are there to crawl through this tunnel?

The Simple
LEAF PILE

This is possibly the easiest "fort" to make.

In autumn, go outside and rake (and rake and rake and rake) up a pile of leaves and jump in them or run through them. You can make small piles of leaves into a maze, seeing who can find their way out first. Just be sure you don't hide in a leaf pile anywhere that a car might be driving!

Nothing to see here! Definitely no kids hiding under here!

Surprise! It's a leaf party, and EVERYONE is invited!

Make a
LOOM TENT

Do you ever get bored living in the same ol' place following the same ol' rules? Why not make a space in the yard to hang out on your own and do things your way?

You can make a tent or lean-to and have a cool hideout that's perfect for hatching adventurous plans, catching some shade on a sunny day, or my favorite activity — napping!

An easy way to start is to turn a low-hanging branch into a loom tent. Take a long piece of parachute cord and use a landscape staple to pin it to the ground about 3 feet away from the branch. Then take the cord up and over the branch, wrapping it around once. Lead the cord to the ground at an angle and pin. Do this again as many times as you like to create a string tent shape. Now weave weeds, grasses, flowers, sticks, and leaves into your loom tent!

Ideas for Backyard Tenting

* **TRICK OUT YOUR HAMMOCK.** Throw an old sheet or blanket over an existing hammock, and hold the sides down with rocks.

* **CREATE A PVC TRIANGLE FRAME.** Work up your design on paper, figuring out how many straight pipes and elbows you will need. Buy your materials, build your frame, and then cover it with a tarp, an old comforter, a rug, or whatever's handy.

* **MAKE A LEAN-TO.** All you need is a wall or low tree branch and some sticks. You can lean sticks that are as tall as you are (or taller) against the branch or wall in a row. You can cover the lean-to with leaves or evergreen branches, or just layer on more sticks until you can't be seen.

BADGER HOLES

Want to tire your little brother out? Ask him to show you how deep a hole he can dig!

A long time ago, pioneers in America dug badger holes to help them stay safe, dry, and alive as they explored new countryside. Badger holes are really just tiny one-room apartments of the simplest design. They could serve for just a night or two, or for an extended stay.

To make your own badger hole, just dig a pit big enough to lie in, all curled up, and then cover the opening of the hole with something. The roof can be anything lightweight: cardboard, branches, a sheet, or a combination of materials. Get creative and try to dig out tiny shelves, steps, pillows, or cubbies inside your badger hole, just like the pioneers did.

Imagine how few options were available to the pioneers who called badger holes their homes. I'm not sure I'd like to live in one in winter, would you?

Dig a hole big enough to lie in all curled up.

Gather leaves and grasses to make the bottom cozy and soft.

What kind of roof will cover your badger hole?

Unexpected
SANDBOXES

Why not make a sandbox out of something you'll be able to reuse for another purpose in the future?

KIDS AND SANDBOXES GO TOGETHER LIKE PEANUT BUTTER AND JELLY. *(The important thing is to not get peanut butter and jelly in your sandbox.)*

At our house, I bought a fabric raised-bed garden bag and filled it with sand. Before filling it, I scattered cinnamon over the base of the bag (supposed to keep crawling insects away) and dumped in a dozen plastic dinosaurs, a large bag of semiprecious stones, and a magnetic dinosaur bone toy kit. Then I filled it up with sand and gave my daughter several small shovels and old paint brushes, so that she could excavate a dig site for a bone the way archaeologists do. This bag sandbox is big enough for her for now, but when she grows out of it I'll use

Men at work, quietly making a small mess.

34

the sand elsewhere in my yard, and she can use the grow bag for its intended purpose — her own raised-bed garden. A molded plastic wading pool can be used this way, too.

AHOY, YE SAND-LOVIN' MATEYS!

If you've got a traditional, store-bought sandbox, why not trick it out? Store-bought sandboxes usually come in two varieties: the turtle and the tugboat. The turtle can easily be ninjafied with the right color of duct tape across the eyes (you can cut out the eye holes or just glue on giant googly eyes instead). You can turn a tugboat into a pirate ship with spray paint that works on plastic. Use a lot of masking tape to cover the top parts and paint the bottom black, the bridge red, and the cover brown to resemble the deck of a boat. You can fasten a plastic pirate flag (the kind that's already fastened to a dowel) to the bridge with zip ties or duct tape.

BEFORE

Cheers to Terry for helping me pull this off the neighbor's curb on garbage day.

AFTER

Happy, sandy co-captains! Arrr!

MAKE A MAP
of Your Neighborhood

You know how some books have a map of mythical places in the first few pages? Why not make your own (slightly embellished) map of your neighborhood?

You can use tracing paper or get paper that looks like parchment, layer it on top of your tablet or device, and gently trace your neighborhood as it's shown in any mapping app.

Make a map and hide it for your friends to find!

Ideas for your mapmaking adventure:

* Use ink from a bottle and a calligraphy pen.

* Mist the paper lightly with coffee or tea to make it look aged.

* Burn the edges of the paper, so that it looks like it's seen battle.

* Measure how far away things are in "paces."

* Use magical versions of local names, like the Realm of Palos Park, the Shire of Willowbrook, the Cal Sag Seas, and the Protected Forests.

* Roll the map up and tie it in a scrap of leather.

* Roll the map up and stick it in a bottle, then cork it and dip the corked end into melted wax to seal it.

* Dig a hole and hide the map underground. (You may need a map to find your map.)

HIDING PLAY MATERIALS

Playing with what you find in nature is good, but sometimes props make play a little something extra.

Where's your little sister going to get all the materials she needs to plan her expedition into outer space, build her time machines, or summon lemonade-bearing fairies? What if she happens to find them (wink)?

When I was a kid we played with whatever we found, which included cigarette packages and old beer bottles (hey, it was the eighties).

When your sister finds the objects and wonders where they came from, be ready to troll her. You might say, "I wonder if that burlap is left over from the early settlers of this area?" or, "Yes, I heard that the previous owner of this house died and left a treasure somewhere on this property — we just didn't know where," and so forth. Hey, it's not lying; it's creating a rich narrative that's probably not true.

Fun play materials you can hide for younger siblings:

* String
* Pipe cleaners
* Fabric
* Burlap
* Buckets
* Tools
* Things to measure with
* Small brooms
* Fake money
* Feathers
* Nails and screws
* Netting
* Yarn and plastic needles for sewing
* Scissors
* Baby wipes
* Mystery objects
* Colored cellophane
* Pieces of plexiglass

Hobos were here!

Money does grow on trees!

Secret nook

Is it a snake or a measuring tape?

Go fish!

Mystery maps

Look under here!

A treasure chest

CHAPTER TWO

PLACES FOR TINKERING

HOW FUN WOULD IT BE TO HAVE YOUR VERY OWN PLACE TO TINKER, so that you could come up with new creations or perform scientific experiments? You could be a mad scientist, a wall musician, or a marble racer! What else could you be, in your tinkering place? Whether you've got a bag of supplies or just a pile of sticks and leaves, you've got what you need to start — your imagination. And remember, as long as no one is getting hurt, there is no right or wrong way to play. Here are some starter ideas for you to explore!

Eli is ready for his audition.

Create a
MUD LAB

How about an activity that gives kids full permission to get muddy and messy . . . *in the name of science?*

"Daycare closing. All toys for sale, including play kitchen $20, desks $10, outdoor balls $5 and toy boxes $5. Woodridge." That was the Craigslist ad that I had been hoping for. I called right away, drove out there, and snapped up a well-used, wood play kitchen. It did not require major surgery to transform it from a regular play kitchen into a laboratory where important scientific research could be done, right here in my yard. I simply painted the kitchen set with waterproofing paint and created a "floor" from an old kitchen counter I salvaged.

GET YOUR GEAR

It doesn't have to be that complicated; any table can be made into a mud lab! Use a kid-height table or bench that can get messy, and lay out some (or all!) of the following:

→ Cooking gear: measuring cups, spoons, whisks

→ Clear tubing

→ Funnels

→ Stones, gravel

→ Food coloring

→ It's important to keep things tidy in laboratories. Use pegboard and hooks to make a lab look professional and inexpensive plastic baskets to keep supplies in order.

IMAGINE THE POSSIBILITIES!

The important part of the lab is really not the kitchen structure, it's the tools that are used with it. We have two American Science & Surplus stores near our house where we shopped for plastic test tubes, beakers, pipettes, tweezers, magnifying glasses, tubes, funnels, hoses, springs, little trays, and pans.

We bought and filled two small, lidded garbage cans, one with topsoil and one with clean play sand. The best part is the tiny lab coat we found that not only would make any kid look professional, but will also keep her somewhat clean.

There is concern in the lab that the results of Hazel's experiment may end up on Lucas's head.

Lucas is locked in on creating an effective antidote to Hazel.

MARBLE RACETRACK

Here's a study in speed, gravity, and fun!

Use ¾-inch clear plastic tubing from the hardware store to make a marble racetrack. You can run the track any-where, indoors or out. Try out different sizes of tubing. Maybe there's one large enough to send a Matchbox car speeding through.

Start by stringing up the tubing. The track can go wherever you want. Try winding it around the stairway banister and through the dog door. A little duct tape or masking tape might be helpful when you test more difficult stunts.

Once the track has been laid, it's time to race. Send the marbles through the track on an incline and see if they stall out or get stuck. Experiment with how high and low you can get the marbles to roll. Try starting the track higher up in a tree and watch whether you can get the marbles to roll all the way down to the ground and then roll back up again.

Jackson knows where the marble goes in, but where will it shoot out?

Hazel moves the hose for maximum marble speed.

Figure out what it takes to get the marble to go all the way to the end with-out getting stuck. Pour colored water down the tube and see if the water stays in the same areas that the marble gets stuck. The best part about this project is that it can be moved again and again and changed up to test angles, inclines, and the laws of physics.

Soda & Mentos ERUPTIONS

Want to make a giant mess? Of course you do!

You can make an explosion using just two materials: Mentos and diet soda. The explosive reaction has to do with the carbon dioxide in the soda (that's what makes it bubbly) and the shape and weight of the Mentos candy. There are tiny air bubbles in the candy "crust" that react with the carbonation in just the perfect way, and that results in an eruption. If you crushed up a Mentos and added it, the eruption would still happen but would be less "whoa."

Here's what you'll need:

* A 2-liter bottle of soda (you can use regular or diet soda, but if you choose to use regular you will get sticky from the sugar and possibly attract every insect in the county, including wasps)

* A package of Mentos (mint flavor has the right "crust")

* A piece of paper

Eli was bold and went without a funnel!

Set the 2-liter bottle somewhere level, away from anything that may be damaged. Roll the piece of paper into a tube, making sure that the bottom of the tube will fit in the mouth of the soda bottle. This funnel will get all the Mentos into the bottle without any spilling. Take six Mentos out of the package, drop them into the soda bottle, and watch the eruption!

Setting BOOBY TRAPS

You can have all kinds of fun defending your fort and keeping tabs on who might be creeping around.

If you don't want your brother messing with your fort, you can set up traps to find out if he's sneaking and peeping. You can make all kinds of traps: booby traps that make noise when an intruder approaches, ones that help prove or track intruders, and traps that are scary or surprising.

You must pay the snack toll for admission!

KEEP OUT

SOME FUN BOOBY TRAP IDEAS

Pull a piece of fishing line (or string) between two objects, like trees, and hook some bells on the line so that when intruders get near it, they set off the bells. Make sure you put the string high enough that you don't trip anybody.

Sprinkle flour in the path in front of the fort and check for footprints.

Place a net (or a piece of fabric) in the tree over the fort. Attach a string to drop down from the net. Tie something to the string that your foe wants. When your foe pulls it, he'll be caught.

Lay bubble wrap out on the lawn. When it pops, you know you have an intruder.

Lay small water balloons on the lawn and cover them with grass clippings or leaves.

Make a SLINGSHOT

Slingshots are old-fashioned shooters, usually kept in your back pocket.

Back in the day, mean kids would shoot pebbles or dried peas. Ouch! I'd rather shoot mini marshmallows into an awaiting mouth (perhaps that of another small human) instead. Or why not try shooting Seedo torpedoes (see page 76) into a vacant lot, pine cones at a tree, rotten apples into the compost heap, or Wiffle balls anywhere?

To build one, you'll need:

* A Y-shaped stick
* Rubber bands
* A small rectangle of fabric or leather with a hole on both ends to act as the actual sling

MAKE IT!

1 Use three large rubber bands to make the sling. Loop one rubber band through both holes in the fabric.

2 Tie the other rubber bands onto each end of the rubber band that's looped onto the fabric.

3 Attach one side of the sling to the Y-shaped branch, using a cow hitch knot. Repeat for the other side.

Try shooting soft treats in the air for your dog. (This dog likes marshmallows!)

COW HITCH KNOT

OK, if I had to have a favorite knot, this is it.

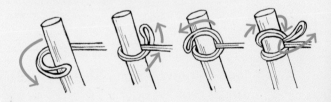

Build a CATAPULT

A catapult is a simple machine that launches things into the air.

An easy first catapult is a lever made with a popsicle stick and a pencil for the fulcrum. Put the pencil on a table and set the popsicle stick on top of it. Hold one side of the popsicle stick down with your hand and load a mini marshmallow on the side that sticks up. Pull the very tip of the marshmallow-loaded side of the popsicle stick down toward the table then let go! Did the marshmallow go sailing? Good.

Let's guess where it's going to land after he STOMPS on it . . .

You can make a bigger catapult outdoors with a few feet of leftover lumber. Use the same idea and design. Lean the piece of lumber over a log or a brick. Load the side of the board that's touching the ground with a bean bag. Now stomp on the side of the board that's in the air. Does the beanbag go flying?

Experiment with different sizes of levers and fulcrums. How much force do you need to throw a pumpkin? Experiment! Does it take three kids jumping on the lever? Six kids? Do you need a longer lever? A taller fulcrum?

You can also splat things like:

* Marshmallows
* Water balloons
* Dog treats (instantly cleaned up if you have a dog)
* Old tomatoes
* Eggs

Protect Your Toys from Pirates!

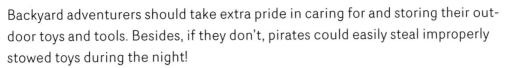

Backyard adventurers should take extra pride in caring for and storing their outdoor toys and tools. Besides, if they don't, pirates could easily steal improperly stowed toys during the night!

THINGS THAT WORK FOR TOY STORAGE

→ Garbage cans with lids (plastic or metal)

→ Outdoor storage boxes

→ Old lidded toy boxes

→ Ziplock storage bags

→ Plastic storage tubs

→ An old file cabinet

→ A mailbox

→ Baskets in a shed

→ Planters and hanging planters

→ Tents

→ Hampers

→ Laundry bags and baskets

→ Bathtub toy corrals

→ Kids' wading pool with cover

Create a WALL OF NOISE

This activity is best for the wee little ones, but everyone (even parents) likes to make a lot of noise sometimes.

Line a fence with thrift-store pots and pans, pie tins, cans, pieces of dismantled toy xylophones, and bells. Nail or screw them on securely. Then pick just the right stick and bang away.

You can also play a memory game. The leader starts by hitting one of the noisemakers, and the other kids follow. The song gets longer with each repetition. For example:

LEADER: BANG

OTHER KIDS: BANG

LEADER: BANG plink

OTHER KIDS: BANG plink

LEADER: BANG plink whaaaack

OTHER KIDS: BANG plink whaaaack

See how long the song gets before someone messes up!

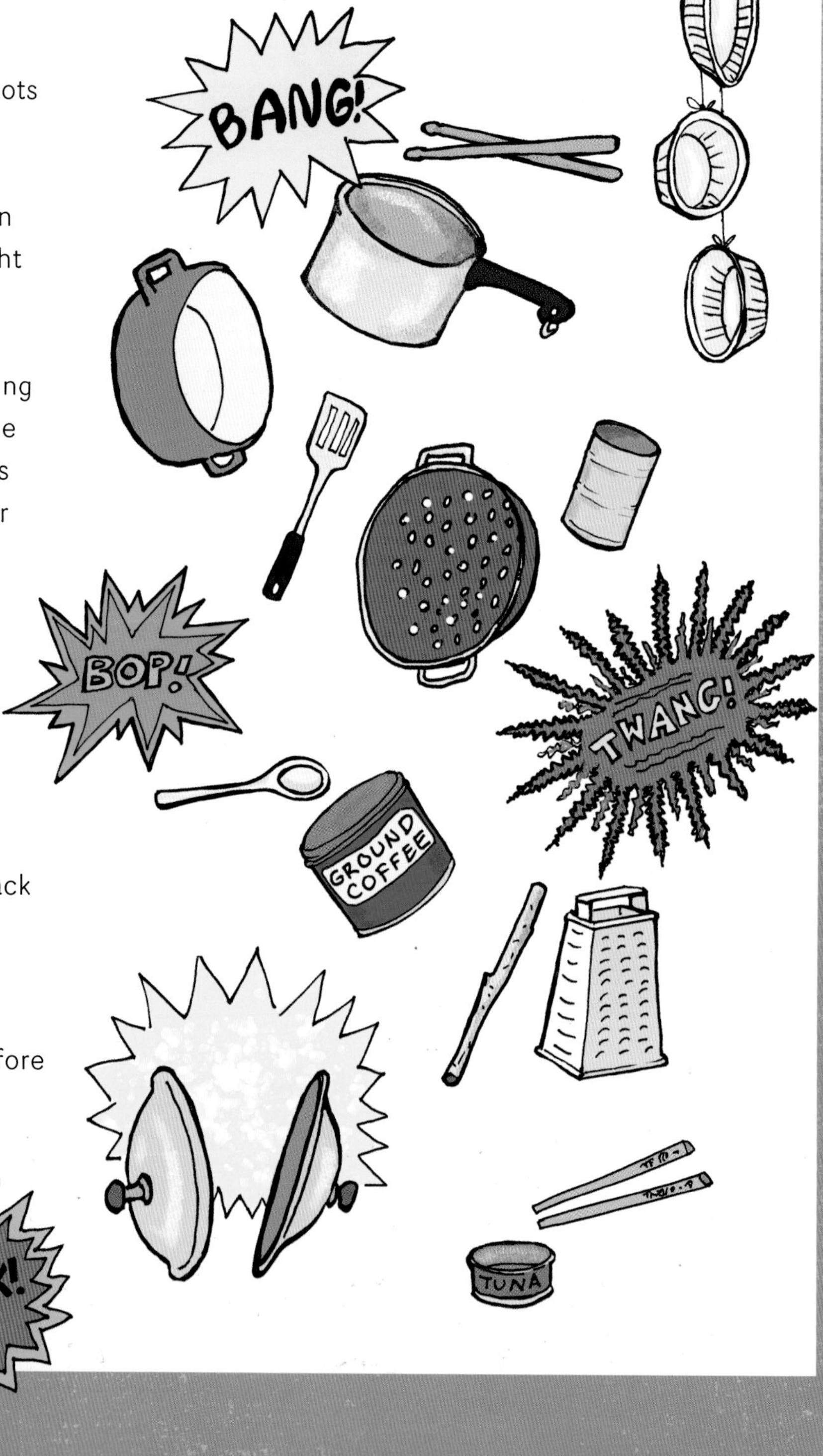

BANG!

BOP!

TWANG!

GROUND COFFEE

WHACK!

TUNA

DIY

RUBE GOLDBERG DEVICE

You can make a complicated machine, and it doesn't even have to do much. Or really anything!

Rube Goldberg was a cartoonist who was famous for making cartoons that feature machines doing very simple tasks in the most complicated way possible — like in the Mouse Trap Game or the first 10 minutes of the movie *Pee-wee's Big Adventure.*

One example would be a machine that you can make, triggered by someone opening the back door of your home (from the inside), that sets off a series of events ending with the door-opener getting hit with a water balloon. Yes, it would be faster and easier to just throw a water balloon at that person, but to do it this way is funnier and takes more creativity.

MAKE A DOG-TREAT-O-MATIC!

1 Kick a soccer ball into a bucket.

2 The bucket is on a pulley that pulls down

3 to trigger a baseball balancing on a piece of wood.

4 The baseball falls down a pipe

5 onto a small lever

6 that spills marbles into a tube

7 that shoot into a pot

8 that gets weighed down by the marbles and

9 pulls a box off the dog treat for the dog!

1 2 3 4 5 6 7 8 9

DOG TREAT

BORED? NO WAY!

There are too many fun things to do!

* Pretend you're stranded on a desert island.

* See what you can make from an old shoe box.

* Try making your own perfumes from flowers.

* Give your little brother a pair of kids' scissors and tell him to go mow the lawn.

* Count how many different bugs you can find and make up names of each (bonus if you draw pictures of them, too).

* Listen to the birds' songs and give them names (the birds or the songs!).

* Decorate a tree and make it feel pretty.

* Learn different knots.

* Throw a handful of change into the lawn and help your friends search for it.

* Blow cubes of Jell-O across the patio with a drinking straw.

* Make a giant nest out of fallen twigs.

* Learn the names of the trees.

* Leave a bread crumb trail like Hansel and Gretel and see what happens to it.

* Plan a parade and enlist the whole neighborhood.

* Make mud pies.

* Make a maze in the snow using just your boots.

* Throw a little bird food near where you play each day. By the end of summer, the birds might know your name when your parents call for you!

* Set up dominoes in the driveway to spell your name.

* Dig as deep as you can.

CHAPTER THREE

NATURALLY WILD

Grow, Eat, Launch, Explore, Create

I GREW UP AS A WILD CHILD and I can't say if it was normal or not for a kid in the seventies and eighties. I just know what I did. When I tell my daughter there were no 24-hour cartoon channels, no one had smartphones or tablets, and kids played outside all day without any adult supervision, she thinks I'm joking. Here is a touch of those times, for a new generation.

Everyone needs a log!

MINIATURE WORLDS

If you could shrink down to the size of your thumb, what would your world look like?

Would it be a magical realm of fairies and gnomes? Would they have battles or live in peace? Or would you live at a racetrack? An airport? Would you live among dinosaurs? Maybe you'd live in a science-fiction scene of alien abductions or planets far, far away?

You can make an imaginary world in your yard pretty easily. Maybe you have some toys that can be left outside to create dioramas, or you can make things like furniture, front doors, or toadstools using moldable plastic beads. Garden centers also carry miniature plants and trees that might look perfect in the tiny world you are creating.

Ragon sets up a tiny tea party.

You don't need a yard to make a tiny world.

Tiny things for a tiny world:

* Aquarium gravel
* Colored sands
* Colored cellophane
* Cardboard and paint
* Air-drying clay and clear sealant
* All kinds of action figures
* Little pieces of fabric
* Old ornaments
* Dollhouse furniture

Grow a
TINY FRUIT TREE

You say tree, I say tiny ammunition factory.

Sometimes I think backyard fruit trees exist solely to grow things that kids can throw at each other. Here in the Midwest, rippled, sour apples and nearly golf ball–size fermented crab apples are the ammo of choice. I imagine in warmer climates, an unsuspecting kid could get an avocado or kumquat in the back.

If you want to grow your own little orchard (for eating or throwing — I'll leave that up to you), maybe try a dwarf fruit tree. They are adorable at 8 to 10 feet tall, and they are truly child-size; you may not even need a ladder to harvest from them.

It can take a while to get a harvest, though — up to 5 years, if you start with a really young tree. Impatient? How about a faster-growing shrub? Elderberries, blueberries, and gooseberries all make great projectiles (and snacks), too.

McIntosh

WHAT SHOULD YOU GROW?

* **APPLES.** You know these! Homegrown apples don't always look pretty like the apples we find at the grocery store, unless they're grown with a lot of chemicals. Ugly apples still taste good, though, and they still make great cider or applesauce.

* **BLUEBERRIES.** Blueberries are easy to grow, if you have the right conditions (a decent amount of sun and well-drained, acid soil). If you can grow blueberries in your area, why not plant three in a triangle and let the center be a fort. That fort will always have the best snacks!

* **RASPBERRIES & BLACKBERRIES.** These grow on prickly canes and spread aggressively. The fruits are too precious to use as ammo — they need to be eaten right away, still warm from the sun.

* **HAZELNUTS.** These cute little shrubs can grow up to 10 feet tall. They'll take 5 years or longer to produce a harvest, though, so plant one now!

* **ELDERBERRIES.** These are the perfect projectiles: tiny enough to not hurt, but stainy enough to leave a mark. Only eat the darkest ones (those are ripe), or cook them first, so you don't get an upset stomach.

FORAGING FOR AMMO

If you're lucky, you may already have a tree that provides projectiles and a source of natural dye. Many urban and suburban neighborhoods are populated with mulberries and black walnuts — two trees you probably wouldn't want to plant, but which you might as well use if you've got them.

MULBERRY TREES are super tall and popular with birds. The fruit is edible, can be fun to mix into secret formulas in the mud lab, and will easily stain clothes a nice purple.

BLACK WALNUT hulls will also stain just about anything they come in contact with. Once you've taken off the outer hull to use for dyeing (use gloves, or you'll stain your hands), rinse off the walnuts and dry them. If you can hammer your way through the shell, you'll find a bit of nutmeat. You'll also get a new appreciation for why walnuts cost so much at the grocery store. Keep in mind that all parts of the black walnut tree are toxic to a lot of normal backyard plants, so be careful when disposing of the hulls and shells.

Natural PAINTS & DYES

Art supplies are all around you!

You can make your own paints and dyes from things found in the backyard. Just grind them up (use fingers, rocks, or sticks) and add water. You can make a brush out of spruce needles, or just paint with your fingers.

Ideas for natural art supplies:

* **LEAVES AND GRASS.** Everyone has had a grass stain, right? Now use the power of grass to make art!

* **DIRT.** Just add water and you've got mud to paint with. What color is the dirt where you live? Where I live, it's almost black. Some places have a deep red dirt that makes a terrific stain/paint.

* **BERRIES.** Elderberries and mulberries are some of my family's favorites.

* **FLOWER PETALS.** How many colors can you create from mashing up flower petals? You might come up with some pretty terrific smelling paint!

MAKE A SPRUCE NEEDLE PAINTBRUSH

spruce needles

string or yarn

stick or dowel

rubber band

1 Secure the needles with a rubber band.

2 Wrap string tightly around them.

3 Paint away!

Grow Your Own
SNACKS

Fruits and vegetables taste so much better when you get to grow and harvest them yourself. Besides, there's just something magical about pulling a carrot out of the ground!

FUN CROPS FOR THE GARDEN

* **THORNLESS FRUITING PLANTS.** 'Raspberry Sorbet' is one thornless raspberry variety — sweet fruits without the pain of getting pricked!

* **CUCAMELONS.** The vine bears tasty, mouse-size fruit and will quickly cover a 4-foot trellis.

* **CHERRY TOMATOES.** These are tiny, sweet, easy late-summer snacks.

One cherry tomato plant will supply enough for practically the whole neighborhood to snack on.

* **CHIVES.** Chive breath is a repellent, though maybe more of a person repellent than bug repellent.

* **MINT.** It grows like crazy and tastes so good!

* **SUNFLOWERS.** Try to eat the seeds before the birds do!

* **LETTUCE.** Why not grow a nonstop salad bar in your backyard?

SNACKS to Identify & Forage

There's food all around you. Why not learn how to forage for your own snacks (somewhere other than in the fridge)? But remember: don't eat anything from the wild unless your parents have identified it!

SOME COMMON FINDS:

* **MULBERRIES.** You can eat the berries. The birds do, too. Then they poop purple poop all over my car. What will happen when YOU eat the berries?

* **ROSE HIPS.** These are so tart!

* **GROUND VIOLETS.** They taste as pretty as they look.

* **CRAB APPLES.** They sure are sour! I think they're better to suck on than to actually eat.

* **SERVICEBERRIES.** They can grow on a bush or tree. They ripen in June (that's why they're also called Juneberries).

* **WOOD SORREL.** You can eat the leaves, flowers, or seed pods. It's all pretty sour!

* **DANDELIONS.** Yes, you can eat those! Give the flowers or the greens a try.

Hazel was told a crab apple was Mother Nature's sour candy, and she fell for it!

Dig Your Own CLAY

People have been making things out of clay for thousands of years. Where do you think our ancestors got the clay? Not at the craft store. You can get it from the ground!

Finding clay in most places is easy. Dig with a hand trowel or regular shovel until you see a layer of light brown clay between layers of dark brown soil. You can also find it where large machinery has been digging or along the banks of a river or stream. What you'll dig up is perfect for making all sorts of cool stuff.

CLAY ARTIST TIPS

→ Mix clay with a bit of water to make it easier to mold.

→ Leave what you make out in the sun, turning it often so it dries on all sides.

→ Your creation will last for a few weeks (or longer if you keep it dry).

→ Try pressing leaves or grass into the clay to leave designs.

→ Make your own paint for your pots out of berries.

MAKE A COIL POT

1 Find enough clay to make a long, thin snake.

2 Coil the snake into a cup or bowl.

3 Smooth the outer sides.

MAKE A PINCH POT

1 Take a ball of clay, then gently press down on the middle of the ball to make a bowl.

2 Keep pressing the sides to make them thinner. Be careful not to push through the clay.

MOWN LABYRINTH

You can make a maze or labyrinth, racetrack, or other game board using only your lawn and a lawnmower.

First, convince your parents to let your lawn grow a little longish, then decide on your design. Maybe start with a simple spiral, like a snail's shell. Or why not mow a chessboard into the lawn and play a giant game of chess?

If you're old enough to run a lawn mower, you could design as you mow. If not, you could mark off the areas for a parent to mow. Remember, you're going to mow the part you walk on and leave the "walls" longer; use string and pegs to mark off the "no mow" areas, then carefully mow the paths. Pick up your string and play until the pattern grows out! When it does, you can just mow a new game into your yard.

SPIRAL

CHESSBOARD

Taking turns racing through the labyrinth

72

LOGS & STUMPS

With a log, you'll never be stumped for play ideas!

If you dropped a large log in a well-used parking lot and put a hidden camera on it, you'd find that hardly anyone who walked near it could resist hopping up onto it for a second. Logs and stumps are free and sometimes plentiful, and there's so much fun to be had with them.

Ideas for log fun:

* Make a path of short logs to walk along. The logs can either be cut side up or lying down. How long will your path be? How far apart should the logs be?

* Use logs to frame a play area or sandbox.

* Create a great climbing obstacle with a small pile of logs. Make sure they are secure and use only enough logs to scramble over.

* Look underneath! A log can have a whole world growing under it. Just roll it away, slightly, and look for the creatures that live underneath it. Be quick, as the bugs will scatter.

Hazel balances on a rotting log.

Looking for bugs in all the right places!

SEEDO TORPEDOES

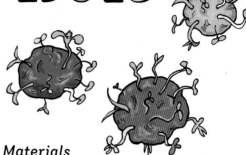

Seed bombs — a.k.a. seedo torpedoes — are projectiles with a beautiful future!

These little balls of shredded newspaper and flower seeds will disintegrate after a few rain showers, releasing seeds that will add flowers to the place where they land. It's an easy and fun way to spread the blooms and beauty. And guess what else? When you seed-bomb a place, you're also spreading plants that feed pollinators and beautify forgotten or hard-to-reach areas (like a vacant lot behind a fence). You could even see if flowers will grow in the crotch of a tree!

Materials

* A blender
* A few sheets of newspaper, tissue paper, or paper towels
* A few cups of water
* Seeds (some suggestions: sunflowers, poppies, zinnias, cosmos, lettuce, bachelor's buttons, nigella) — or a wildflower mix
* Food coloring (optional)

MAKE IT!

1 Rip up some old newspapers and soak them in warm water.

2 Put the paper in a blender.

3 Add a cup or two of warm water.

Whiz it up!

Pour that goo into a large bowl. Fill a small bowl with the seeds you're going to add to the seedo torpedoes.

Take a handful of the goo and squeeze it lightly in one hand, letting the extra moisture dribble off. Flatten the goo slightly so that it's covering most of your palm.

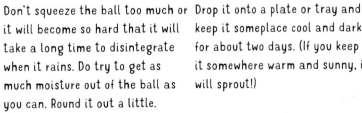

Grab a few seeds with your dry hand and drop them in the middle of the flattened goo. Crunch this mixture together so that you seal the seeds inside the middle of the ball of goo in your hand.

Don't squeeze the ball too much or it will become so hard that it will take a long time to disintegrate when it rains. Do try to get as much moisture out of the ball as you can. Round it out a little.

Drop it onto a plate or tray and keep it someplace cool and dark for about two days. (If you keep it somewhere warm and sunny, it will sprout!)

DRUMS

Do you love to bang on things?

Why not create a place to drum away in your backyard? You could either use parts from a beat-up old drum set, or (if those are hard to find) see what kind noises you can make with old pots and pans, jelly molds, buckets, tubes, and pipes. Anything that sounds great when you whack it will work!

Our yard features a taken-apart kids' drum set. We found it at a church rummage sale, and when we got it home we realized that it was missing a part that kept it all together. Since we'd spent a whole five dollars on it, we weren't about to give up. So we stuck all the drums among plants in the garden, where they can be banged on every day. The drums have been out there for a few years and look just as good as they did when we purchased them. We also hung some cymbals from a tree branch using a piece of knotted nylon rope. They're fun to bang on (but not light enough for the wind make them clang).

She was born to be the drummer in a punk band. Keep practicing, Ragon!

BE CONSIDERATE

Before you make a racket, it's nice to check in with your neighbors. For example, you don't want to be banging on drums while someone who works the night shift is sleeping, during a newborn's nap time, or if someone has an anxious dog.

You can also baffle (block) sound with thick fences and by planting lots of tall grasses and shrubs (each blade helps to deaden sound). Using soundproof foam (or something like it) on surrounding fences helps, too.

CHAPTER FOUR

SETTING UP CAMP

GOING CAMPING IS A MAGICAL EXPERIENCE, BUT IT CAN ALSO BE HARD WORK. Why not hone your camping skills in your backyard before you set out for a week in the woods with no water or electricity? There's plenty of nature in your backyard, and the fire-roasted marshmallows will taste just as good as they would in the far-flung forest.

How many s'mores can Max eat before not feeling so great? We should find out soon.

BACKYARD CAMPING

Rough it, kid!

So you and your friends want to go camping by yourselves in the yard, huh? Get prepared for the big time (that's overnight) by trying a few of these exercises:

* **STAY OUTSIDE.** Set an egg timer for 3 hours and don't go indoors for anything during those 3 hours. When you do go in, write a list of the things you wish you'd had with you.

* **TAKE A TECH BREAK.** Camping means no screens. Can you power off for 3 hours?

* **PLAN AN OUTDOOR MEAL.** Write a list of everything you'll need to make your meal and imagine every step involved in preparing and eating your meal. (See page 91.)

* **TRY TAKING A MIDDAY NAP IN THE YARD.** Find a spot where you're protected from the sun, lie down, and listen to all the sounds of the neighborhood as you're falling asleep. Think about how it might sound different at night.

Memphis serenades the neighborhood.

* **PLAN FOR ANIMAL ENCOUNTERS.** What kinds of nocturnal animals live in your neighborhood? Racoons? Possums? Make a plan for how you'll deal with animal visits during the night.

el chupacabra

(FAKE) NEIGHBORHOOD LORE

Invent your own urban legend.

There's usually one haunted house in the neighborhood, but if there isn't, no one is saying you can't start the rumor. Do you think your little brother would buy it? To avoid hurt feelings, though, it may be best if the potentially shunned neighbors are in on the game. Some people might really enjoy the role of spooky neighbor!

On Halloween night, your make-believe neighborhood folklore can become an opportunity for that neighbor to ham it up. What will they do? Lie in wait to scare trick-or-treaters or hand out full-size candy bars to prove it's not true?

Neighborhood points of interest you could invent:

* The person who lives in that house is a giant.

* That's where the inventor of the Power Rangers lives!

* Did you know that house was built by Abraham Lincoln?

* Old Man Johnson's house is haunted by cats.

* There's an amusement park in the backyard of that house, but the owner can't stand kids. Too bad!

* That house is made out of sugar cubes.

* That house is run by talking dogs.

Make a HAND-WASHING STATION

Playing hard can be dirty business.

Make an outdoor hand-washing station, so that you don't even need to come indoors to clean up!

All you need is:

* A bar of soap
* The legs from a pair of old pantyhose or tights
* A gallon jug of water
* A screwdriver, knife, or other pokey thing

It's nice to stop and clean up a little before getting dirty again.

MAKE IT!

1 Insert the bar of soap into one leg of the pantyhose and tie a knot just above the soap.

2 Poke a few holes in the lid of the jug.

3 Tie the leg to a low-hanging branch. Hang the jug from the same branch, using the other leg of the pantyhose.

Create an
OUTDOOR SHOWER

Getting dirty is hard work, but getting cleaned up again doesn't have to be.

Why not design your own outdoor shower? There are many different ways to set one up.

* You can rig up a watering can on a rope or use a hose with a spray nozzle and a pump.

* Or you could take an even simpler route: fill a few ziplock bags with water, hang them from a low branch, and poke holes in them.

* Easier still: hang up a shower curtain and wait for a rainstorm!

MAKE A FOOT-WASHING STATION

It's certainly easier to wash your feet than to clean your whole body! To keep from leaving muddy footprints all over the house, put a foot-washing station outside the back door. Fill an old tire or a milk crate with large river pebbles and hose yourself off while standing on them: the water and muck will just drain away.

Sometimes just your tootsies need a good hosing off.

Set Up an
OUTDOOR TOILET

Who has time to go indoors to pee? Not you!

Why not set up an outdoor toilet? You could either buy a camping toilet or make your own. To pee in private, set up a small pop-up tent for your toilet, or build a tepee (get it? "TePEE") around it.

You can easily turn a 5-gallon bucket into a camp toilet. Fashion a seat out of a pool noodle: just cut it to size and put a lengthwise slit in one side, so you can slide it on the bucket.

Fill the bucket partway with sawdust, moss, or cedar shavings, to act as absorption material, and add more each time you use the toilet. When your bucket is full, dig a hole and dump your bucket into it; that'll be your dedicated human waste compost area. You can use straw, sawdust, or grass clippings to cover up fresh deposits.

Sometimes you just can't hold it long enough to get into the house.

Or put your pee to work! Pee may work as a critter repellent or compost additive, so pee around the perimeter of the yard or into buckets and you can spread that sunshine!

PICK YOUR OWN TOILET PAPER

Burdock leaves make great toilet paper, as do mullein, lamb's ears, and maple leaves. Make sure not to use anything that will ruin your day, like poison ivy, stinging nettles, or giant hogweed. It's also best to avoid anything small, ferny, or grasslike, and anything super glossy, like wild ginger (they just don't absorb).

BURDOCK

MULLEIN

LAMB'S EARS

MAPLE LEAVES

POISON IVY

STINGING NETTLE

GIANT HOGWEED

FERNS

GRASSES

GLOSSY LEAVES
(Wild Ginger)

Make a FIRE PIT

If parents aren't around, or you're not sure it's safe to have a real fire, why not build a make-believe one?

When I was little, we made a ring of stones, piled up twigs in the center, and pretended we were barbecuing our victims over it. With no safety hazards or rules to obey (other than not throwing rocks), imaginary fire pits can be set up anywhere and make great centerpieces to secret hideaway meeting spots!

If you do want to have a real fire, though, here are a few things you and your parents will need to do:

* **MAKE SURE YOUR TOWN ALLOWS CAMPFIRES** and learn what regulations might apply. Some towns only allow fires in a store-bought fire pit. If you live in a dry or drought-stricken area, skip the campfire. You don't want to be the one to start the next wildfire!

* **MAKE A FIRE RING.** Choose a spot that is protected from the wind and at least 15 feet away from any plants, structures, or low-hanging branches. Remove all grass and twigs, clearing a 10-foot area all around the fire pit. Dig a pit about 1 foot deep and at least 2 feet wide. Circle the pit with rocks.

Bubble, bubble, toil and stay-out-of-trouble with this pretend campfire.

* **BURN SAFELY.** Make sure you have buckets of water or a hose handy in case of emergencies. Keep your fire small, and allow it to burn out completely (or douse it with water) before you leave the scene.

HOBO CAMP FOOD & OLD-TIMEY COOKING

Everything tastes better when you eat it outdoors.

When I was a kid, I'd play outside so much that I didn't know what time it was and I would forget to eat. My mom would just leave a peanut butter and jelly sandwich on the back steps for me to eat whenever I remembered I was hungry. If you're going to be out in the yard for awhile, you can pack sandwiches, fruit, and pre-made lunch packs in rodent-proof boxes or coolers, and you won't even have to go inside when you get hungry.

FOR A REAL TREAT, COOK A MEAL OVER A CAMPFIRE!

The easiest place to start, of course, is roasting hot dogs on a stick (preferably a stick you've foraged yourself).

Try roasting these on a stick:

* Toast
* Pineapple
* Peach slices
* Bacon
* Biscuit dough
* Apple slices sprinkled with cinnamon and sugar

MAKE A QUESADILLA ROLLUP

Quesadillas are easy to cook over a campfire.

1 Cut a large piece of aluminum foil, lay down one tortilla, sprinkle with cheese, and top with the second tortilla.

ALUMINUM FOIL

2 Roll it up in the foil and set it near the fire to cook.

3 Check it occasionally and eat it once the cheese gets ooey-gooey melty.

DON'T COOK THAT CAN!

A long time ago, hobos and other people used to cook canned foods on campfires using the can as a pot. They would just open up the top of the can, place it near the fire, and cook until the contents were warm. Nowadays, we know that heating cans causes toxic substances to leach into food, so don't put cans of food in your campfire!

MAKE A S'MORE CONE

For dessert, you could make s'mores, or you could try my favorite variation: the s'more cone! Fill an ice cream cone with marshmallows and any number of different fillings. Wrap the filled cone in aluminum foil and set it near the fire. Once the insides become totally melted, bite right in or dig out the innards with a spoon.

For fillings, try:

* Nutella
* Bananas
* Sprinkles
* Strawberries
* Oreo crumbles
* M&M's
* Blueberries
* Apples
* Chocolate
* Caramel pieces

OUTDOOR STAGES
for Performances or Fomenting a Rebellion

"Look at me!" shouts every kid, ever. Here's the chance to be in the spotlight, for real!

In addition to being ideal for putting on performances, kid-size stages make the best meeting places, a great "home" for games of tag, and a natural place for cake to be delivered to a waiting birthday girl. With enough imagination, any area can become a stage.

The best stages have a little raised platform (you can use your porch or you can make a platform with pallets, plywood, or sturdy cardboard). Make sure that your stage is safe enough to hold several actors that may or may not stomp around a lot. You'll also need a curtain for dramatic entrances (try

Really, there's no one hogging the stage here.

hanging a shower curtain from a tree branch or making a PVC frame for it) and seating for the audience. Benches and chairs will work, of course, but so will straw bales, stumps, and logs.

MAKE AN EASY PUPPET THEATER

If you're not up for building a stage, you can make a puppet theater. It's easy to make one from an old cardboard box, fabric, and branches, or from old picture frames. Why not make a miniature theater for bugs out of sticks and stones? I bet the bugs would enjoy a minuscule opera or tiny monster truck rally!

94

CHAPTER FIVE

SIDEWALKS, FENCES, AND DRIVEWAYS

A.K.A. Places to Draw

YOUR YARD ISN'T JUST AN OUTDOOR SPACE; IT'S A BLANK CANVAS, JUST WAITING TO BE USED. You're surrounded by a potential outdoor art gallery, and you probably don't realize it! Whether it's the driveway, the front sidewalk, or the fence that surrounds your yard, any flat surface can become a place to draw.

Life is better with colorful fences.

GRAFFITI
on Fences

Whatever kind of fence you have — vinyl, split rail, chain link, picket, or stockade — there's a way to turn it into a play space.

If you're lucky enough to have a large solid fence, you can really have fun with it! After all, no one can see it but you and your family. Why not paint it with a few coats of chalkboard paint so you and your friends can draw murals every day? All you have to do to wipe away yesterday's artwork is hit it with the hose.

STRING DESIGNS

If you're not up for a lot of mess, there are other ways to use your fence as a creative play space. Tack tiny nails to a wood fence to make string designs. You can change up the designs whenever you feel like it. If you have a chain-link fence, you can weave anything you can find through the fence — from branches to ribbon to leftover spaghetti.

Henry and friends are hard at work making (and unmaking) designs with yarn.

SHAVING CREAM & CHEESE PUFFS

Here's another fun activity. Smear dollar store shaving cream all over the fence and see what you can use to make designs. Add leaves, cheese puffs, seeds, pine needles, grass clippings, and newspaper. When you're done, you can just hose it away.

Cheese puffs and leaves are all you need to create a work of art.

Spray the fence, not people!

GLOW IN THE DARK PAINT & SQUIRT GUNS

If you want to go a little more extreme, why not try out other kinds of paint? Tempera paints wash away easily when you've put away the brushes for the day. Glow-in-the-dark paints and black light–reactive paints (if you think you'll ever use a black light outdoors) are fun for after-dark adventures. You can even fill a squirt gun (or several!) with paint and see if you can make shapes or write names while standing on the other side of the yard.

SPLAT!

Fun on the
DRIVEWAY

Your driveway has a billion possibilities.

Not only is it great for biking, skating, scootering, skateboarding, and rolling balls, it's also perfect for painting, chalking, drawing, playing, and creating miniature explosions. Everyone can pitch in to clean up the driveway after playtime is over.

Ideas for driveway play:

* Draw a town or village with sidewalk chalk.

* Draw a Pac-Man game and decide which of your friends get to be Blinky, Pinky, Inky, and Clyde.

* Make up your own board game and draw the game board on your driveway.

* Create mosaics out of petals, sticks, and dried beans.

* Set up a racetrack.

* Pretend it's the tarmac at the world's busiest airport and you are a plane.

* Hold a car wash or pet wash.

* Play field hockey.

* Use paint rollers and water to roll out designs, then watch them dry. Zero clean up!

* Play hopscotch.

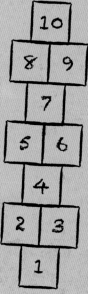

CHALK OUTLINES

A bucket of sidewalk chalk = hours of entertainment (or at least *one* hour).

You and your friends can take turns lying down and having your outlines traced in chalk. You can also experiment with tracing the shadow of a kid who's standing instead of lying down.

From here, you might have a mystery to solve. You can make up a backstory about who this person was, what she was doing in your driveway, and where she is now. You can also draw clothes and accessories on the outline.

Try tracing two at a time.

I'd recommend choosing a comfortable position. But fine, have it your way!

Check out that awesome sidewalk style!

Hazel's chalk outline cracks us up.

EXPLODING
SIDEWALK
CHALK

Here's a science experiment wrapped inside a fun, colorful project.

It's a take on the old vinegar-and-baking-soda rocket bottle. When it's done, you'll have piles of foamy color in the driveway that you can paint with, and, best of all, it's easy to wash away.

Here's what you'll need:

* 8 tablespoons baking soda
* 2 paper towels
* 4 small rubber bands
* 2 cups vinegar
* 4 quart-size ziplock plastic bags
* 2 cups cornstarch
* Food coloring

1 Make packets for the baking soda by cutting each of the paper towels into four squares and sprinkling about 2 tablespoons of baking soda into the center of each square. Roll the squares up and wrap them with rubber bands.

2 Mix the vinegar with the corn starch. Divide the mixture evenly among the four plastic bags. Add several drops of food coloring to each bag.

3 Take your bags and packets outside to the driveway or sidewalk. Shake the bags to mix, then add a baking soda packet and quickly reseal the bag. Step back!

4 Watch the bags puff up, then explode! Use the exploded paint as liquid sidewalk chalk.

Noah and Ragon can hardly contain their excitement (or their exploding chalk!).

CHAPTER SIX

ADVENTURE COURSE

HAVING SOME FRIENDS OVER FOR A BIRTHDAY PARTY? Try setting up an adventure course! It can be as long or as short as you need it to be and as messy and gross as you like (at our house, we make it as gross as possible, in case you were wondering). Parents can participate or just watch — but the kids should decide which. You can use stuff you already have in the garage, or you can pick up a few inexpensive things a couple of days before the party. Maybe your whole family can decide on the sequence of obstacles and set it up in the yard the day of the party, together! Here are a few other jumping off points (get it?) to add to your backyard adventure course (or to use as a stand-alone adventure!).

Honestly, a little mud never hurt anybody.

SWING IT!

Old-school tire swings are a fun way to reuse tires.

You can easily buy a kit online to make a tire swing, or you can find the pieces and make one yourself — the way kids have been doing it ever since tires were invented.

Here's what you'll need:

* One regular tire
* 50 feet of 1½-inch rope
* A length of old hose or tubing (to protect the tree from rope-burn)
* Optional: a heavy screw eye, carabiner, or swivel (these come in the purchased kits)

Ragon is brave, strong, and not afraid of heights.

OTHER KINDS OF SWINGS

Is the tire too much fuss for you? You can just have a rope swing, of course. Or set up two ropes the same way as for the tire swing and make a regular swing with a plank seat. You can also drill a hole in the middle of an old skateboard deck, thread the rope through, and tie a knot. Now you have a skateboard practice swing to practice your rad moves and balance.

CHOOSE THE RIGHT TREE. You'll need a tree with a large branch that's not going to snap on you, so try a sycamore, oak, or maple. The tree shouldn't be near anything you could crash into while swinging. You should use a branch that is at least 6 inches in diameter and tall enough for excellent swinging action but not so tall that you need a helicopter to get the rope over it.

SELECT A SOFT SPOT. Make sure the area underneath the swing is soft enough to cushion any tumbles. A level, even patch of grass is best.

PREPARE YOUR TIRE. Use a regular tire, not a heavy duty one, and check for any exposed steel belt or damage. Drill holes (or ask your parents to) in what will be the bottom of the tire swing, so that rain doesn't collect and create a place for mosquitos to breed. You might also want to paint the inside of the tire sky blue, to discourage hornets from building nests in there.

HANG THE ROPE. Thread the part of the rope that will touch the tree through a piece of hose or tubing to keep the rope from rubbing against the branch. Use a ladder to reach the branch, put the protective tubing in place, and tie the rope using a bowline knot. Tie the other end of the rope to the tire, so that the tire is as far off the ground as you like. Your swing should hang just far enough from the trunk of the tree that you'll never crash into it, but not so far down the branch that the branch itself begins to weaken.

HOW TO TIE A BOWLINE KNOT

Here's the knot you need for hanging a tire swing.

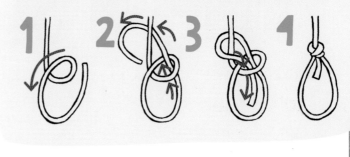

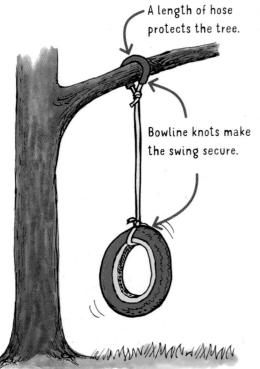

A length of hose protects the tree.

Bowline knots make the swing secure.

Ragon is having a swinging good time! →

109

Make Your Own
SLIP 'N SLIDE

Let's make a total mess. We'll talk about it for *months*, but maybe we should do a little prep work first?

Slip 'N Slide is the brand name of a long piece of slippery plastic you tack down on your lawn, spray with water, and attempt to slide on. Really, though, you can use any old sheet of heavy-duty plastic or tarp that holds water (has zero holes), and you can add different kinds of liquid to your homemade slippery sheet and see what happens. You may not even need a slope. And even if you make a big mess of yourselves, you can always just hose off!

Max is about to go SPLAT!

SLIPPERY SUBSTANCES

→ dish soap

→ baby oil

→ dollar store shaving cream

→ water balloons

→ poster paints

→ slime

TOUGH LI'L MUDDERS

The shortest route from here to there is through this tunnel, over that slime, around that pile of sticks, and ... hard to see with this pie in my face!

Use garbage cans, tools, tape, yarn, tires, and thrift store items to make a steeplechase (obstacle) course. Take turns running through it. You can have two teams or you can use a stopwatch to time one person running through. First, dream up different obstacles. Here are some ideas:

BABY BOUNCING
Bounce to the finish line on toys made for little guys.

MOMMY IS A MUMMY
Wrap a mommy up like a mummy using toilet paper.

BROOM HOCKEY
Use a coconut, a nearly deflated ball, an old stuffed animal, or other wonky-shaped item.

SNAKE PIT
Dig for plastic snakes in the mud pit.

THE CRUNCH WALK

Lay down two rows of Hula-Hoops and run through them like they're tires in a military obstacle course. You can even add gross things inside the hoops to step on, like snack foods, Jell-O, mud, or water balloons.

THE TOOT SEAT

Sit on a whoopee cushion placed on a chair.

WHOOPEE CUSHION

KIDDO ROLL

Climb inside a clean plastic garbage can and get rolled by your partner for a few feet.

BOZO BUCKETS

Line up a series of laundry baskets in a row and take turns throwing a ball or bean bag into them, starting with the one nearest to you and working your way to the one farthest from you.

MAZE MADNESS

Make a simple maze using stakes along with a roll of fabric, butcher paper, or newsprint paper. Arrange stakes into a spiral and wrap the fabric around your framework. Put the materials needed for the next challenge (like a ball or beanbag) in the center so the kids have to run in and out again quickly.

SNAKE TUNNEL

Crawl through a tunnel filled with plastic snakes.

EGG TOSS

Throw an egg at a partner — underhand throws only, and never aim at a person's face. (Hint: at our house, I hard-boil half the eggs so that they never break!)

PIE FIGHT!

Fill dessert-size paper plates with shaving cream to throw at people. You could use whipped cream, but shaving cream is less attractive to bees and pets, and if you buy the "sensitive" kind, it doesn't hurt if you get some in your eyes. (Although it doesn't taste very good!)

Make Your Own STILTS

Back in the old days, before television, movies, or even radio, kids would have fun for hours making and playing with stilts.

You can make these yourselves! The easiest stilts to make require two clean, empty aluminum cans (like the kind tomatoes or peaches come in) and two long pieces of strong rope. Try it out! Can you walk on stilts? Most kids 100 years ago could!

MAKE THEM!

1 Use a drill or church-key can opener to poke two holes across from each other at the unopened end of the can. (Ask an adult for permission or help.)

2 Thread a piece of rope through the holes.

3 Tie knots where your hands hit the ropes to make it easy to hold on.

SAFETY TIPS

It might be a good idea to protect yourself when you're learning to walk on stilts, just like you do when learning to roller-skate or ride a bike. Wear long-sleeve shirts, long pants, closed-toe shoes, and socks. Also wear a helmet, knee pads, and elbow pads. Gloves aren't a terrible idea, either.

Red Yarn
LASER CLIMB

How sneaky can you be?

Have you ever watched a television show or movie where a spy is trying to steal something major and they have to climb, leap, limbo, and slide around a seemingly impossible maze of red laser beams without setting off the alarm?

Here's a way to reproduce that as a harmless backyard activity (without the alarms).

For this activity, you'll need a ton of red yarn and some landscape staples.

Tie one end of the yarn to a tree branch, then lead it, zigging and zagging all around the protected area, tying onto other trees, fences, or poles as you wish. Use the landscape staples to hold the yarn down to the ground when needed. You can up the ante with an object that's being protected, like a hockey trophy, giant tinfoil ball, or any genuine giant diamonds you have lying around. Put that object in the center of the red yarn maze. Have someone try to grab it and then get out with the object. It makes it harder to move when you're holding something, especially if that thing is irregularly shaped.

Step it up:

* Tie tiny jingle bells to some sections of string, to set off the "alarms" when the string is touched.

* Saturate sections of red yarn with red paint, so that you're marked red-handed if you deny touching the beams.

If the red yarn touches you, your turn is over.

CARDBOARD ARMOR

Use old cardboard boxes to make a suit of armor!

* You can cut out pieces and make them fit together, or you can just cut open the tops and bottoms, and slip inside and roll on the ground until the boxes are pliable.

* You can make duct tape suspenders very easily.

* Cut eyeholes in a smaller box to use as a helmet.

You can be a medieval knight or an evil robot — or a medieval, evil robot knight.

* Use bubble wrap to protect limbs.

And make sure that no matter how much armor you cover yourself with, it's still possible to easily use the bathroom!

CHAPTER SEVEN

WATER, BUBBLES, AND GOO

PLAYING WITH WATER IS MAGICAL, COOLING, AND FUN. Water play is a fun activity for the whole family. Even tweens and teens who hate everything enjoy a refreshing blast on a hot day. (Too bad doing the dishes isn't as fun.) Here are a few water play ideas to get you started.

With all this soap and water, I wonder if we can skip bath time tonight. Just kidding — we are totally skipping it.

SPRINKLER SETUPS

Why is it so much fun to get wet in the sprinkler? Is it even more fun to make the sprinkler, too? Let's find out!

No one would turn down the chance to play in a regular old store-bought sprinkler, but you can have fun making your own sprinkler out of household items. Why not try punching holes in a soda bottle or a pool noodle and duct-taping it to the hose? If you want to get really crafty, you could design and make one using PVC pipe.

POOL NOODLE

SODA BOTTLE

PVC PIPING

Kids and lawns grow quickly with regular watering.

Make a WATER BLOB

This is easier, cheaper, and more fun than it looks. It gets 6 out of 5 stars.

Here's an inexpensive project that doesn't take long to make and can be customized in countless ways. Also, it's not a very permanent plaything. It'll start to leak the longer it's jumped on. This somehow makes it more fun to play with, because you're also causing destruction! This is a great activity for summertime birthday parties.

Here's what you'll need:

* Heavy duty (4 mm) plastic sheeting (get a very large piece, as you're going to fold it in half)
* Duct tape

1 Fold the piece of plastic sheeting in half.

2 Seal the three open sides with duct tape, leaving only a small opening so you can fill it with the hose.

3 Fill your blob with water. You can also add fun stuff to the blob, including bath toys, food coloring, or soap.

4 When the blob is full of water, take the hose out and seal up the opening with tape. For extra slippery fun, squirt some dish soap and water on it and slide around.

Additional add-ins

* Biodegradable glitter
* Paint
* Food coloring
* Soft bath toys
* Bits of colored sponge

SUPER SOAKER!

Squirt away the afternoon!

Squirt guns were invented to be filled with water. But why stop there?

Try filling a super soaker with:

* Water and food coloring

* Paint and water

* Egg salad (just kidding)

* Half water/half white vinegar — try to shoot targets of baking soda (what happens next?)

* Organic fertilizers so that you can soak all the plants in your yard and help them grow

* Water with fragrance, like almond oil or mint extract

Kids really should only shoot other kids who are armed with squirt guns.

Don't want a squirt in the eye? Next time, wear swim goggles.

BABY POOL FUN

The baby pool is fun for more than just water!

Things you can fill a baby pool with:

* Water balloons
* Slime
* Frozen peas
* Jell-O
* Glitter
* Gelli Baff
* Pistachio pudding
* Shaving cream
* Popcorn
* Angry lobsters
* Sand
* Seedo torpedo goo (see page 76)

* Blankets and pillows
* Straw
* Feathers
* Ranch dressing
* Jingle bells
* Water beads
* Grass clippings
* Plastic snakes
* Real snakes
* Ball pit balls
* Shredded paper
* Autumn leaves
* Legos

* Pom-poms
* Gumbo
* Cheese puffs
* Pizzas
* Foam packing peanuts
* Gummy bears
* Topsoil + water = mud
* Gum balls
* Pillow stuffing
* Mashed potatoes
* Worms

PIÑATA
Full of Water Balloons

Piñatas are the best!

But squabbling over candy and toys is the worst, especially on a super hot day. So why not create a little surprise and fill a piñata with mini water balloons?

You can use a water balloon filler from the store to fill and tie them up quickly or you can do it the old-fashioned way and fill and tie them one by one. You may need to reinforce the hanger on your piñata, as it will become very heavy!

If the successful batter is wearing a blindfold, as is traditional, she won't know what hit her!

 If they knew what was inside, would they be standing so close?

HOW TO MAKE A PIÑATA

1 Blow up a regular balloon.

2 Make a paste of two parts flour to one part water. You may have to add more flour or water to get a sticky, paste-like consistency.

3 Tear up pieces of paper into 4" to 6" strips.

4 Using your hand, smear some paste onto the balloon.

5 Add strips of paper over the goo until it's covered.

6 Goo, cover, and repeat.

7 Let dry overnight.

8 Using a knife, pop the balloon inside and cut a flap for adding a filling.

9 You can make holes to string it and hang it, or you can make a string "basket" to hold it if it's very heavy.

Make
GIANT BUBBLES

Bubbles are always fun for everyone! And giant bubbles are twice as awesome.

The secret to making giant bubbles is an additive called glycerin, which you can find at craft stores, pharmacies, or online. It's worth finding and adding because it helps make giant bubbles!

Mix your bubble juice in a small bucket or large plastic bowl, using:

* 6 cups water

* ½ cup Dawn or Joy liquid dish soap (it has to be an old-school dish soap, as newer and more-organic brands add foam-cutting agents)

* 2 tablespoons glycerin

Scarlett is a bubble-blowing champ!

Ways to make bubble frames:

* Thread a 6- to 7-inch piece of string through two drinking straws. Hold a straw in either hand, dip in bubble solution, and blow gently.

* Cut a 5-foot-long piece of cotton string. Tie it into a loop. Take two long branches (about the same length) and tie the loop onto the branches using two small pieces of yarn. It should look sort of like a pair of old-fashioned TV antennae with a loop tied on in the middle. Dip in solution and run!

* Cut off the bottom 2 inches of a water bottle and fit a sock on the end of the bottle. Dip the sock in the bubble juice and blow into the other end. What happens?

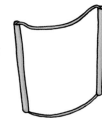

TYVEK SUIT
Full of Water Balloons

Tyvek coveralls are a favorite way to play around here. Usually they are to protect you from getting dirty, but not the way we play!

White Tyvek contamination suits are inexpensive and available in the painting section of your local hardware store. Some of them come with hoods and even booties. Sadly, they don't come in children's sizes, but almost any school-age kid can wear the small or extra small sizes. You can tie the wrists and ankles (or use rubber bands) if the suits are super baggy.

Hazel's legs are so heavy, she can't take even one step.

If there are more kids than suits and it's a hot day, you can form two teams and take turns sliding mini water balloons into the suits and see who can fit the most inside. It may require wiggling, shimmying, and accidentally popping some balloons (that's part of the fun).

Once both teams have one kid with a suit full of water balloons, dare them to hug it out or whatever else it takes to pop the water balloons.

As soon as Hazel figures out that if she can't move, Max can't move either, she knocks him down like a sack of potatoes.

EGGSHELL PAINT BOMBS

Just crack, fill, and SPLAT!

If your family is game to crack eggs a little differently than usual when cooking, you can accumulate many of these potential paint-filled projectiles. The thing is to crack one end of the egg with a pin, then keep picking at the hole with the pin until it's just large enough to drain the egg innards. Once the shells are empty, rinse them and let them dry.

When the shells are dry, you can fill them with with finger paints or tempera paints. (Make sure whatever paints you use can be washed off with water.) Keep the eggs upright in the egg carton until you're ready to take them outside and throw them at the driveway, fences, or trees. The eggshells will compost into the lawn and the paint will wash away, so if you miss a couple of spots when you clean up, it's no big deal.

Noah has the look of someone who is up to no good.

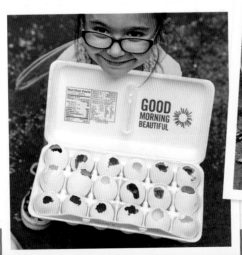

Ragon is READY!

CHAPTER EIGHT

IT AIN'T OVER YET

AFTER DINNER AND BEFORE BEDTIME IS THE PERFECT TIME to slather on the insect repellant and go run off the last of the day's energy. If there's a bath on the agenda before bed, it's also a great time to make a mess! Around here, after dinner is when all the neighborhood kids come out to play.

We can party all night, or at least until bedtime.

Old-Timey
YARD GAMES

Here are some fun games your parents probably played when they were kids. Now you can, too — day or night!

RED ROVER

You need an even number of kids for this one, preferably six or eight. Let's say you have eight kids, so that's two teams of four. One team shouts "Red Rover, Red Rover, send Edie right over!" Then Edie needs to run as hard as she can toward the other kids, who are standing in a line with arms linked. If Edie can break through the linked arms she gets to steal someone from that team and take them to her original team. If she doesn't make it through, she has to stay on the team she tried to run through.

Variations

This game can hurt. An easy variation is for the running kid to slip under locked arms instead of breaking through. If he is blocked (not overly forcefully) by the team with locked arms, they get to keep him.

KICK THE CAN

No supplies other than an empty can are needed for some of the best outdoor fun around! Place the can in a central location. Whoever is It counts to twenty while the other kids scatter and hide. The can is "safe," so kids try to run to and touch the can before It can catch them. If It tags you, you are captured.

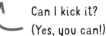
Can I kick it?
(Yes, you can!)

I think the best part of this game is when it's going so fast that the person trying to touch the can so that they are safe ends up kicking the can with It running right behind them. When the can gets kicked and moved, it can provide other players an opportunity or put them in more danger. The first player captured is It next time.

Variations

* The can is a plastic cup full of paint.

* Play at night with everyone wearing glow sticks, so they're easier to find.

* Use the whole neighborhood (with your neighbors' permission), so that it becomes very difficult to find kids and It is lured far away from the can.

"Mother, may I leap like a leopard?"

MOTHER, MAY I?

"Mother, may I pretend it's 10 after 11?"

Mother, May I? is like the inside-out version of Simon Says. Instead of Simon giving orders, the players all start out in a line and take turns asking Mother how many steps they can move up. If they forget to ask, "Mother, may I move up three steps?" and instead squeal, "Can I move up three steps?" they have to take steps backward. When they reach Mother (which is entirely up to Mother, as you'll notice), they get to switch positions. This is excellent play for power-hungry kids.

Variations

* Make the shyest kid in the room Mother.

* Incorporate messy activities, as in "Mother, may I spray Silly String on the kid next to me?"

* Create a mud or paint trap between the kids and Mother that they have to cross.

Turn Dolls into
MUMMIES

You can turn any toy into a mummy, but dolls are the creepiest — especially at night.

All you need is some toilet paper, paper towels, and flour-and-water paste mixed in a bowl.

Wrap the "deceased" with toilet paper until it looks like a proper mummy. Cut strips of paper towels, dip the strips into

them. Make sure to cover every inch, then let your mummy dry. Now, you're ready to decorate it with markers.

Will you bury the mummy? Create a tomb or pyramid from bricks? Hang it from a tree to keep strangers away?

DUCT TAPE ZOMBIES

This is a totally normal project for totally normal families. Definitely nothing strange going on here on these pages. Nope.

This project takes at least two people to make: a person who gets wrapped and a person to do the wrapping. It helps if more than one person works on the wrapping, though.

First step: pee. The person to be wrapped needs to use the bathroom before this gets underway, as there will be no bathroom breaks for a while. The wrapped person should also wear old clothes that will be okay if they're accidentally cut with scissors. It's good to wear clingy clothes, such as a long-sleeve turtleneck and leggings or sweatpants tucked into socks.

Start wrapping! The wrapper will wrap the other person from neck to toes in plastic wrap so that every inch is covered, then quickly move into wrapping duct tape over the plastic wrap. (A handy tip: I've found that dollar store duct tape is difficult to peel and tear as it's very thin; it's much easier to work with better duct tape from the hardware store.)

Fast and loose. It takes a long time to wrap a person in duct tape, so it's important to be quick in your work. Also, don't wrap too tightly! Cover the other person's whole body in duct tape.

Free the inner child. When you're done wrapping, carefully cut down the back to free the person from the tape. Be careful not to cut their clothing. Cut straight down to their heels and see if they can wiggle their feet out. Once the wrapped person is free, you can both work on taping over the cut you just made.

What to do with your zombie:

* Pour sand in the zombie's feet to keep it upright. Fill it with expanding spray sealant foam to keep it from being crushed.

* Wrap it with gauze and ripped sheets (you can even dye them with tea to make them look old and decrepit).

* Dress the figure in clothes.

* Get a head: Try foam wig heads, fake pumpkins, old masks, beach balls, or any kind of head you can make out of papier-mâché.

GLOW STICK HUNT

Let's stay up just a little bit longer!

It's been a long summer day of play, and it's late now, way after bedtime. Your little brothers are lying in bed after a bath and three bedtime stories and you suddenly yell, "GET UP! GET UP! There's one more thing to do!!" Then send them outside on a hunt for glow sticks hidden around the yard.

It's best if the glow sticks are strung on cords so the finders don't need bags or baskets for collecting them, but can just wear their findings around their necks. Once your brothers start glowing instead of the yard, it's time for them to go back to bed. For real this time.

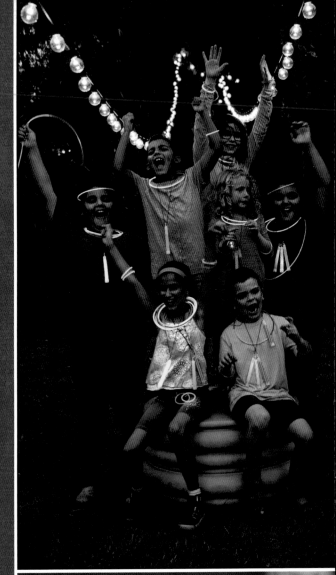

FLASHLIGHT TAG

You know how to play hide-and-seek already. Here's a fun way to play it at night without things getting too spooky.

First, play Rock, Paper, Scissors to see who will be It. The kid that's It gets a flashlight, turns around, closes his or her eyes, and counts to 20. All the other kids scatter and hide. The kid who is It has to find the other kids, but It doesn't have to touch them to catch them — It only has to shine the flashlight on them for them to be caught. The first one caught is the next It.

It's good to decide what boundaries your group should use before playing and decide how far is too far so no one gets left out there, unfound, and eaten by werewolves.

SUPER SECRET SECTION

★ FOR PARENTS ONLY! ★

Usually rules are for kids, but in this book they're for the PARENTS. Here are some ground rules for you to keep in mind. Remember, while everyone is outside having fun, Mom and Dad have to unplug, too.

SET THEM FREE!

Do you want your kids to learn about risk taking? Have strong and healthy bodies and minds? Do you want them to learn to love nature? Feel confident fixing problems by themselves? I can't think of much I wouldn't do to make those things happen for my kid.

Free play is the answer.

Now that so many kids are overscheduled and cherish screen time above all else, unstructured play has decreased, and, with it, boredom has also decreased. Boredom, however, is an important catalyst to creative, imaginative play. Boredom is good. Boredom leads to making magic.

By finding ways to provide extended periods of uninterrupted, completely imaginative outdoor play, we are doing a world of good for children's social and emotional intelligence, risk-taking abilities, sensory processing, and anxiety levels. To me, the benefits of

encouraging, facilitating, and creating a space for outdoor play are so much more important than having a perfectly green lawn.

SET THE SCENE

How often do you actually use your outdoor space? Is it just a place for your dog to "go"? Do you often eat dinner outdoors? Enjoy your morning coffee on the patio? Entertain out there? Most yards I see are sorely underused for any purpose except the dog. Why not give up hopes of pristine yardkeeping and let it be a playroom for your kids?

To further convince you, let's make a little spreadsheet

listing how much all your lawn-maintenance costs are per year. Then multiply that cost by how long you expect to live in your house. Chances are, it's a ton of money. You can save all that money in a coffee can in the cupboard and spend it on the lawn and patio of your dreams once the kids are grown.

As someone in the landscaping industry who thinks people have lost perspective in recent years, I'd encourage you to put up some tall fences (to keep kids in boundaries and minimize noise), mulch your entire yard with wood chips (the cheapest, most cost effective and worry-free surface), and let your kids go to it. Let them play.

PLAY HOWS

"Play is often talked about as if it were a relief from serious learning. But for children play is serious learning. Play is really the work of childhood."
— Fred Rogers

LET THEM TAKE RISKS AND BE UNCIVILIZED.

Unscripted, uncivilized, and wild free play is what sculpts little humans into awesome adults. This is where risk taking, project management, self-regulation, daydreaming, and emotional development come together to build a stronger child in both body and mind. And it costs us exactly nothing.

Studies have shown that kids who spend extended periods of time in free play have more self-control than kids who spend more time in adult-directed play (lessons, sports, classes, and other organized activities). In recent years, extracurricular activities, electronic devices, helicopter parents, and a lack of places to romp have chipped away at the free play that formerly existed in schools (recess!) and at home.

LET THEM GET MESSY!

"Sensory play" is just a new term for messy play. Messy play is important for kids, especially young ones, because it's full of discoveries. It also stimulates both their gross motor skills (the larger muscles, like arms, legs, and core) and fine motor skills (things like fingers, wrists, and toes). During this type of play, kids learn to focus and to work with other kids to get things done — all while having fun and exploring new ideas.

Letting go of backyard norms can be hard for lots of parents, so take it one step at a time. An activity that might help soothe that anxiety is getting your kids a play wardrobe. You can just relegate some of their existing wardrobe to a special hamper or basket, or shop at garage sales and thrift stores for clothes that can get messy or stained. Maybe even buy a few smocks, lab coats, aprons, raincoats, and the like. Waterproof boots are a wise investment, too. Backyard adventurers of a certain age can learn to wash and care for their own outdoor clothes. They can even learn to mend them.

WAIT FOR AN INVITATION.

Kids need extended periods of play with no expectations, interference, or structure. But they still need adults to set out the paints for them, teach them how to use tools so they can build with them, and attend the show they spent days creating and rehearsing. However, adult participation in the activity itself should always be by invitation only. Let the kids have their little realm as they are discovering that they are not helpless.

RE-LEARN HOW TO PLAY

> *"A child loves his play, not because it's easy, but because it's hard."* — Dr. Spock

Sometimes messy, self-directed, outdoor play is a pretty foreign concept to the whole family. Parents have to let go of the idea of having a perfect backyard (whatever that is), a desire for constant tidiness, and the need to keep a constant eye on their children. Kids need reassurance that it's okay to be messy! Kids can develop anxieties about making messes — after all, we've asked them not to smear Nutella on the sofa 30,000 times. Now we're encouraging them to make much bigger messes than that.

A comfortable place to start may be to hold a scavenger hunt where adults have done all of the set up, but the kids are left to solve it. This still feels adult-directed, but really the hunt will be what kids make of it. It's okay to have things go in unexpected directions, for an activity to turn into something totally different. In fact, it's better than okay. That's where real magic happens!

Remember that it's okay to let kids be bored. Boredom is exactly what sparks imagination, and you need a good chunk of time for boredom to turn to magic. Free play doesn't really start for almost an hour after kids begin playing, so block out a day, a weekend, or a school vacation to do nothing but make messes, unplug, and discover.

LEARN OTHER STUFF, TOO

Wild, outdoor free play is really great for learning other things too — like science, technology, engineering, and math (teachers call those STEM subjects for short).

SCIENCE: This is easy! There is no place better than the outdoors to explore botany (plants), earth sciences, soil studies, ornithology (birds), zoology (animals), entomology (insects), meteorology (weather), astronomy (the sky and stars), horticulture (gardening and making things grow), and geology (rocks).

TECHNOLOGY: By playing outside and discovering how things are built and how they work, kids learn the foundation upon which technology is built. Learning how to tell the time from the sun, how to make simple machines, and that things fall apart are other technology-related lessons kids can learn from play.

ENGINEERING: From messy outdoor play, kids can learn how to make simple machines or gadgets and how to go back to the drawing board (over and over again) when their creations aren't working exactly as they'd like. Older kids can build contraptions in the backyard based on their own drawings, measurements, and designs.

MATH: Playing outdoors all day requires a lot of problem solving, and that includes using math. Kids have to make sure they have enough of their required materials, and will spend time measuring things and sorting (once things are sorted, they need to be counted, right?). Building confidence in these kinds of everyday math situations helps foster a love of math further down the line.

DON'T BE STUFFY

It seems that many people try to make the outdoors a lot like the indoors by sanitizing it or organizing it. I'm pretty sure this isn't what nature has in mind for us.

If an area is neat as a pin, where are the discoveries to be made? My family was recently in a backyard that was so tidy we were afraid we were going to mess it up. The turf was perfectly green and lush, with no weeds. I didn't want my kid to even step in that grass. It takes untold chemicals (herbicides, fungicides, insecticides, and fertilizers) to get a lawn to look that way, and I happen to like

all of the fungus that grows on my kid.

In addition to having a tidy but toxic lawn, the yard felt like it was more for show than for play. There were no fences, making it seem like we were inches away from the neighbors the whole time we were there. I was afraid that if we tossed a ball around it could land in someone else's territory. The patio was stone and off of the west-facing back of the house, so it was too hot to sit there. There were no mature trees for shade or interest. The home's owners only use the yard twice a year for backyard barbecues, and it's so hot at those barbecues that guests always want to hang out inside. Kids naturally didn't want to use the space for play and I don't blame them.

GET WILD!

Who is your backyard a habitat for?

Lots of people have special gardens to attract butterflies. They research what butterflies like to eat in different stages of life and plant accordingly. Some people grow specific plants that birds like to eat, such as coneflowers for songbirds and trumpet-shaped blooms for hummingbirds. I've even seen gardens with little houses for toads and special homes for bugs to overwinter. I don't often see people planting special

gardens or creating habitats for kids (other than the standard swing set). Why not?

I wouldn't say that butterflies, birds, toads, and bugs aren't awesome (because they are) but aren't human kids totally the best? Are we spoiling kids if we give them fun yards to play in, with found objects or dirt-cheap toys to play with? Are we giving them too much when we make them unplug and get themselves outside to play in the mud?

If your glass is half full and your yard is half empty, why not surrender some of that space as a wild habitat for your favorite native mammals? Save the kids!

HOW WILD CAN YOU GO?

It's cool to have a yard with a function. It shouldn't just sit there as a showpiece. But if you decide to let it get a little wild, how wild will you go?

STOP MOWING THE LAWN. If you currently have a lawn and just stop mowing it (if your neighborhood allows), it won't really get that wild right away — just thick. It'll make great tunnels for cars and toys. To go wilder, you might need to remove some lawn and add natives or wildflower seed mix. Eco-Lawn is a great grass seed mix that is drought tolerant (once established), super tough, and doesn't need to be mowed.

It's very fine and soft and is a perfect texture for kids to play in and on.

KiLL YOUR LAWN ALTOGETHER.
Wood chips are a perfect play base layer. They're also fantastic at lawn-killing (or just beating back the weeds). If you've got hard-core smothering to do, you can put down a thick layer of newspaper or old bed sheets before you start piling on the wood chips. The best part is that wood chips are often free from your municipality or your local arborist. Score!

MAKE THE WiLDNESS LOOK iNTENTiONAL.
What if people think it looks too wild? My first suggestion: add a mega-manicured mini-hedge (such as boxwood) around the mayhem to make it look intentional. Or try adding a perfectly clipped conical bush, front and center, as if to say, "I know what I'm doing here and I'm perfectly able to do it." You can also get your backyard certified as a natural wildlife habitat from the National Wildlife Federation. With that you get a little plaque that states that letting the area go wild is good for plants, water, bugs, animals, and kids.

Also, as Robert Frost said, good fences make good neighbors.

IDENTIFYING AND ELIMINATING REAL DANGERS

Before serious play can begin, you'll need to scout your yard for possible dangers. Not all dangers need to be removed, since outdoor free play is not about sanitizing a play space for kids. You should, however, discuss any major danger concerns with the kids and set some guidelines before turning them loose.

Here are some guidelines:

* Scout for poisonous plants, like poison ivy, nightshade vine, or yew. Remove plants with poison that spreads by touch (poison ivy, hogweed) and educate kids about plants that are poisonous by ingestion (yew, castor bean).

* Identify sharp or decayed items in the yard and other sources of danger. Are there old rusty fence posts in your yard? A decaying bridge? Set the ground rules for all areas of the yard, including the danger zones.

* Decide on rules for what can be thrown and what can't. May kids throw wood chips? Berries? Snowballs? It's up to you.

* Is anyone in your neighborhood allergic to bee stings? If so, plant flowers, which bees love, far away from play

areas. It's also important to teach kids to respect bees (and other bugs).

* Talk about property lines and trespassing. Meet the neighbors. Explain to them that they are living near a kids' discovery zone.

* Install fences or plant trees and shrubs to contain the wildness.

SUIT YOURSELF

There is no one style of yard that suits all families. You need to figure out what your family's needs are and determine how to work with them. I have a really big yard that's very open, so I created a wood chip–covered play area right off the back of my house where I can keep an eye on my young daughter as she explores by herself. When she's older, her needs will change and we'll make a new plan. The important thing is to make the space functional and fun, whatever age she is.

Elements to consider including in the backyard:

FENCES. With a good fence, not only do you have privacy, but you also have no pressure to keep your yard in surgically clean order. A good fence can also help with noise control.

WOOD CHIPS. Often free from your city or town, wood chips can keep unwanted weeds down. Wood chips also help create better soil as they compost.

SYNTHETIC GRASS. Sometimes the most sustainable thing to do, especially in drought-stricken regions, is to stop trying to grow grass and just fake it.

VEGETABLE GARDENS. Give kids a place to snack from and to learn how to grow their own food.

PLACES FOR OUTDOOR CRAFTS. A picnic table or something similar works well. You'll want someplace great to carve pumpkins or to make a piñata.

SHADE SAILS. Large triangles of fabric can be stretched and anchored to buildings, trees, or poles to create shade where there isn't any.

PET USE AREAS. You don't want dog poop commingling with your kid's play area.

A BIG, BOUNCY THANK-YOU TO:

Hazel and Dan Thomsen. Cheryl Lynn Tomlin. Dayle, Sofie, Sadie, and Max Joiner. Julie, Matt, and Memphis Render. Krista and Elsie Reilly. Cyndi, Mike, Merritt, William, and Joseph Moloney. Amy Van Aalst, Henry and Eloise Brinkman. Nicole Suarez and Ragon Crowder. Megan, Elijah, and Noah Drozd. Kara, Vince, Grace, Eli, Scarlett, and Greta Fanelli. Karla and Anaïs Nunnally. Kate, Julian, and Lucas Galbincea. Douae and Ameen Mohammed. Charlotte, Rachel, Josh, and Sarah Sacks. Cari Dale, Travis, Caiden, and Kellan Vogt. Hillary and Bishop Remis. Lydia, Koda, Avalon, Rowan, and Weslie Ng. Alissa and David Rindfleish. Brian Helfrich and family. Aquascape. Lynn Petrak. Susan Crosby. Wahoo Woods/Dundee Township. Kourtney Sellers. Jessica Armstrong. Carleen Madigan. Ilona Sherratt. Jeaniette Goodlow. Elizabeth Montville. Tom Crouch. Amy DiDominicis. The Children's Farm. Debra Middleton. Krista and Jackson Carter. Eric, Mikey, and Addy Podlasek. Palos East Elementary School.

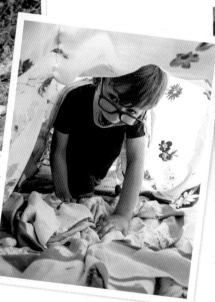

EXPLORE, LEARN, CREATE!
WITH MORE BOOKS FROM STOREY

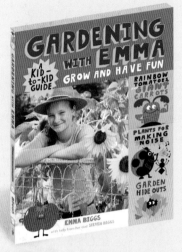

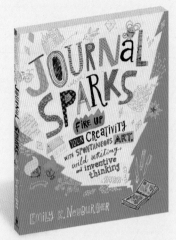

by Emma Biggs, with Steven Biggs

With tips for how to grow a flower stand garden, suggestions for veggies from tiny to colossal, and ways to make play spaces among the plants, 13-year-old Emma Biggs offers original, practical, and entertaining kid-to-kid gardening advice and inspiration.

by Emily K. Neuburger

Make a visual day-in-your-life map, turn random splotches into quirky characters for a playful story, and list the things that make you *you*! These 60 interactive writing prompts and art how-tos will help spur your imaginative self-expression.

by Jonathan Adolph

From water fireworks and soda stalactites to a caterpillar hatchery, a balloon barometer, and much more, you can conduct these 40 fun, foolproof, and fascinating science experiments in a glass canning jar.